STEPPING STONES
to Change

ANTOINETTE SPURRIER

Stepping Stones to Change

Copyright © 2015 by Antoinette Spurrier

All rights reserved. No part of this book may be reproduced or transmitted in any form or by any means without written permission of the author.

ISBN: 978-0-9903824-6-1 (paperback)

Dedication

This book is dedicated to:

Christian Francis

Connor Scott

Francisco Reynoso

David Scott

Each and every one of you has contributed generously to my life.

Contents

Introduction 1

1 Aligning Your Dual Natures:
  The Limited Self and the Eternal Self 3

2 Stepping Stones to Change 27

3 Manifestation: From the Inside Out 79

4 Creativity.................................... 87

Acknowledgments

Collaborators

Andrew Freedman,
wordsmith who was the keeper of the intention; he expanded the book in scope, vitality and heart.

Jacqui Freedman,
artistic contributor who captures Spirit and Nature in her light-filled watercolors. Her work is available through Jacquifree@yahoo.com

Sherry (Heidi) Hall,
the woman with the velvet voice and empathetic heart, who gave inspirational input.

Deborah Probst Kayes,
proofreader, coordinator, sustainer, and multi-tasker with extraordinary tenacity and patience.

Becky Lawton,
provider of multifaceted contributions.

Suresh Ramaswamy,
creative webmaster for FieldsOfLight.com

Anne Marie Welsh,
editor and dynamic catalyst for the birthing process of *Creating Deliberate Happiness: The Complete Guide* and this series.

Mark Murphy,
aka Mr. Creativity who provided graphic art input and inspiration.

Special Mention

The Foundation for Personal and Spiritual Empowerment
FieldsOfLight.com

The San Diego Foundation

Yvonne Gorder Christenson for her artistic contributions.

My gratitude and appreciation also go to: Martin Anthony, Dr. James Ajemian, Rebecca and Todd Astill, Dr. Concepcion Barrio, The Bectold Family, Lou Bewersdorf, Wendell and Elaine Blonigan, Sheila Byrne, Renee and Sophia Carson, Cathi Eggleston, Joseph Escoffier, Susann and Richard Fishman, Christian Francis, Paul Gorsuch, Norma Grey, Kari Kashani, Nikki Mann, Sandra and Geoffrey Mavis, Deirdre Maher, Alvada and Weston Maughan, John McLaurin, Patrick and Catherine McNabb, Anne McQuillan, Kevin McQuillen, Ron and Marlane Miriello, Dr. Carl and Chris Murphy, Chaitanya Narayan, Jim and Kathleen Newcomb, Brian and Emily Quinn, Francisco Reynoso, Ginger Palmer, Jan Saucier, Connor Scott, Jeffrey Spurrier, David and Rose Spurrier, Ann Summa, Lisa Baker Scurr & Ron Scurr, Ricardo Torres-Roldan and Family, Penny Wing.

In Memoriam

John Laurence,
teacher, mentor and spiritual advisor. He was blessed with spiritual gifts that he shared unselfishly with others. He was instrumental in who I have become.

John McLaurin,
who personified friendship and sustained constancy, loyalty and love in that friendship. We journeyed together in the past and will do so again.

Linda Provence Diehl,
a beloved friend who expressed in wonderful ways both analytical thought and intuitive knowing. She made everyone feel that she had the ability to be mother to all.

Charles Mirandon,
who contributed through his friendship and loving support of our family and projects for decades.

Introduction

To the Reader,

My desire is to inspire powerful transformation that can lead you to lasting happiness—deliberately. The process begins when you look inward and begin to make fundamental changes in your own consciousness. This book will guide you through the process by describing the spiritual principles that underlie any such transformation and providing a series of Eight Stepping Stone techniques, including affirmations, to help you change. These practical tools can result in personal and spiritual empowerment and lead you back to your natural state of joy.

A fuller account and detailed analysis of the background to these practices is available in my *Creating Deliberate Happiness: The Complete Guide*, a book that explains more fully the natural patterns and scientific laws governing psychological and spiritual growth.

In this smaller volume I focus on a sequence of principles, and then on practical techniques that, with patience and persistence, will bring the results described:

- A definition of success, health and wealth that focuses beyond the material to a deeper awareness of your Divine nature.

- An exploration of the limited ego-based consciousness vs. your true spiritual nature and the power of affirmations to integrate the two.

- Techniques to uproot negative self-talk and alter long standing feelings of worthlessness that sabotage love and happiness.

- A practical, realistic focus on the Stepping Stones to Change to help overcome negative thoughts and behaviors that may confront you when you try to make lasting change.

- An explanation of manifestation and how, when you overcome any negative undertow, you can manifest love, abundance, spiritual empowerment, creativity and lasting happiness.

I wish to help you claim yourself through self-understanding and proven techniques in personal transformation. As you better understand spiritual law and these Stepping Stones, you will become a co-creator with the source of all creation. And you will eventually return to your natural state of happiness. Congratulations on taking the first step!

Antoinette Spurrier
San Diego, California

Angel Holding a Baby
By Yvonne G. Christenson

CHAPTER 1

Aligning Your Dual Natures:

The Limited Self and the Eternal Self

The Essence of Happiness

The subject of happiness is so profound that it is written about in the world's great literature as well as in its eminent spiritual traditions. The pursuit of happiness is a fundamental right, referenced in the U.S. Constitution. It is a driving force that underlies our ventures and adventures in this physical world. Happiness also can be intensely consuming and powerful in and of itself.

But why do we pursue happiness? Why do you? Is it simply a reflex to avoid pain, or is it a distinct drive to access a greater, higher state of pleasure? Is pleasure simply experienced at the physical and psychological levels, or could there be a state of transcendent pleasure that is tied to our spiritual nature?

In chapter 1 invite you to reflect on the nature of true happiness, to challenge self-defeating ideas and to embrace a new sense of your deservedness and self-worth. The key to this process and to the how the eight stepping stones will unlock for you the state of lasting happiness and joy comes in understanding that you are two selves, an Eternal being of infinite light and love and a Limited self living in the material world of ego drives. Spiritual practices will help you to align and integrate those two selves. We will cover these related topics as well:

- The art of happiness: not what you find, but what you create.
- Your entitlement to more happiness.
- Self-exploration and journaling as a technique.
- Preconceptions about happiness.
- Ideas that limit your access to more happiness.
- Self-knowledge and awareness of your spiritual essence.
- Hidden happiness contracts.
- Steps toward creating greater happiness.
- Happiness in terms of a deeper relationship with yourself.
- Changing consciousness to change your circumstances.
- Obstacles to happiness.
- Feelings of Self-worth and Deservedness.
- Introduction and exploration of the Limited Self.
- Introduction and exploration of the Eternal Self.
- Conflict between these two selves.
- Eternal Self's natural state of happiness and joy.

The need for happiness seems so basic, so deeply intrinsic to our natures, yet it remains elusive. Our efforts to "find" happiness are usually misplaced, and we "find" only transitory happiness on the material level—a vanishing specter of possibility. But when we come to understand our dual natures, human and divine, and then experience and integrate them, we can begin to experience self-empowerment and then lasting happiness, and finally joy, our native state.

So for you, as for all of us, your dilemma is that you possess those two selves; they are in frequent communication, yet function in nearly opposite ways. This is not an abstract philosophical quandary; it is a pervasive reality. If you are not consciously aware of these two selves, your attempts to achieve peace, harmony, and happiness become more complicated. Yet mankind's deepest expressions of philosophical and religious thought often refer to this internal duality. Present-day author and psychologist John Welwood puts it succinctly: "To discover our human wholeness….we need to bring the two sides of our nature— absolute and relative, supra-personal and personal, heaven and earth— together at last." This integration offers hope for healing the schism and finding inner peace and happiness.

The Two Selves Defined

Let us take a deeper look at these two selves and how they operate in a polarized consciousness. For the sake of this discussion, let's call one self the Limited Self, identified and bound by the physical form, mind, feelings and the culture in which it lives. The other, the Eternal Self, expresses our spiritual nature, our true unchangeable essence.

Put simply, the Limited Self consists of:

- Your chemical, biological nature, operating in the physical dimension under physiological laws.

- Your psychological layers of mental consciousness, operating within a social context.

- Your beliefs and life experiences, operating within your environment and culture.

- Your extraordinary ability to evaluate, interpret and assign meaning to your experiences, literally defining yourself through your imagination.

Because we seldom view the interface between these four aspects, our Limited Self may feel compartmentalized, incorrectly interpreting experiences and events, wrongly imagining ourselves as body identified,

> *Awakening is when the eyes of consciousness open so that consciousness begins to see what is real, instead of consciousness seeing only an illusion, or what it wants to be real.*
>
> JOHN DE RUITER,
> *Dialogues with Emerging Spiritual Teachers*

continuously changing, impermanent beings.

Even though the Limited Self is unaware of its spiritual potential, it nonetheless carries the capacity for joy within. However, fragmentation, conflict, and persistent habits of thought—including the habit of worry, circular negative thinking and defeating self-talk—become impediments on the road to happiness and self-awareness.

Your other self, the expansive Eternal Self, is your true spiritual nature, pursuing nothing, for its state of consciousness is joy transcendent. That Self, your soul nature, is always aware of the actions and activities of the Limited Self; your soul is the watcher over your ego. And this spiritual essence can manifest in subtle, powerful ways as the expression of who you truly are.

All physical life contains the movement of Divine Intelligence through the vibratory law of creation. As humans, we have an innate capacity to unfold through developmental stages into multi-faceted beings with highly advanced, complex thoughts, vivid imaginations, sparks of divine creativity and the ability to plan and achieve goals. Part of the miracle of our lives is that our magnificence in this form will never come again in exactly the same place, in the same way. Each of us is unique in the Universe. YOUR individual expression is unlike anyone else's.

Unfortunately, we generally go about life unaware of our infinite potential, for we are focused primarily on three-dimensional reality. We access knowledge through our bio-chemical nature and filter experiences through the individual persona, or ego. The five senses, as necessary as they are in helping us navigate this physical dimension, are like a twelve- inch ruler. They can measure the "fiber and texture" of the material world, but they cannot reach or measure Infinity.

Relentless forces of change assault this Limited Self, for nothing stays the same in this world. Even the semi-permanent values and mores of society are in a constant state of flux. As the world spins around us in an ever-chang-

> *The inner battle is between our lower self, or pseudo-self—the body identified ego—and our true higher self, the soul, the image of God within us.*
>
> PARAMAHANSA YOGANANDA

ing panorama of experiences, our lives are impacted in ways great and small. Events happen, and we interpret and assign meaning to them. This capacity adds both to the wonder and the complexity to life. More often than not, our interpretation of events is subjective. Fundamentally, we place a fog—a kind of conceptual overlay—onto our experiences and then make an emotional investment in that overlay, taking it to be "real" in and of itself.

But all of us also have an innate ability to reflect on ourselves, a trait that lends resilience to us because our ability to interpret and imagine can open a door to new interpretation and redefinition. We can restructure the meaning we see in the physical dimension. "Consciousness is imaginative, sensitive and pliable; it can think and dream itself into any state," wrote Indian scholar and sage, Paramahansa Yogananda. He is referring here to our amazing ability to re-create ourselves, to change and transform consciousness itself.

While the capacity for self-motivated change is always present, the Limited Self is more often changed by biological or psychological conditions that continually impact it. It is altered by the hands of circumstances and the clay of environment: childhood and our early upbringing, genetics, and diet are just a few of the influences that continually impact this Limited Self. With such a constant bombardment of uncertainty, where there is really no telling what may happen in the next moment, is it any wonder that the Limited Self feels powerless against the law of change?

Stranger O' Self

Stranger o' Self
Dream Self gone wandering
Among the ruins of time
Gone to find self meeting self
Yet strangers always.

Stranger o' Self
Viewed from countless mirrors
Reflectors of false images
Self seeing self
Distorted on a mirror of glass.

Unknown substance
in search of form.
Stranger, Dream Self
Gone wandering
Among the ruins of time.

To operate entirely from the Limited Self makes the pursuit of happiness a precarious journey. "The only constant, is change," wrote the Greek philosopher Heraclitus. We do indeed live largely in a world of unending change over which none of us has true control.

But even when we assess ourselves through this limited, changeable self, we can continue to define, redefine and interpret. In my counseling work through the years, I have seen clients who awaken to their intrinsic capacity to choose new perspectives, and then are able to reframe even the most difficult memories and experiences. This is a profound truth that will be reinforced throughout this book.

Until we claim that power to choose, and until that choosing comes from our more enlightened, expanded Eternal Self, our perceptions will be constrained by the Limited Self's view of reality. What we see, hear, sense, feel and therefore experience, is filtered through the mind with all its pre-conditioning. We begin to believe our thoughts and perceptions are real, regardless of their origin. Roger Walse, in his "State of the Integral Enterprise: Part 1," wrote: "What is crucial to recognize is that all perceptions reflect perspectives, and all perspectives are partial and selective. Each perspective both reveals and conceals, clarifies and distorts. However, perspectives and perceptions do not clearly reveal their own limitations."

> *Happiness is inherent in oneself and is not due to external causes. One must realize one's Self in order to open the store of unalloyed happiness.*
>
> RAMANA MAHARSHI

Assumptions and perceptions can harden into beliefs, which can manifest, consciously or unconsciously, as behaviors. It is imperative, therefore, that we learn to recognize how this process of self- definition operates.

As long as limiting beliefs remain unknown and unconscious, we remain a puppet, pulled by the strings of conditioned behaviors or false concepts of ourselves. As a result, we will continue to experience a limited range of happiness. Fortunately, at our best, we naturally strive to go beyond such limits; we want to experience ourselves as integrated and whole.

Personality is Ego-driven

Our personality, as delightful and creative as it may be, is limited to the perceptions of mind and body alone. Its drives are primarily based on preservation, survival, the elimination of pain, finding pleasure, and satisfying the senses, none of which, as we have seen, can provide true happiness. Nature intended for the ego-based personality to survive, reproduce, and endure. The emphasis of this ego-based personality is thus always upon the "I," which has little capacity to extend beyond itself to the needs, the necessities, the wants and desires of others.

Our human experience creates a kind of hypnosis in which we identify with the Limited Self. Jean Paul Sartre, the French existentialist, wrote: "Everything happens as if consciousness were hypnotized by this ego which it has established, which it has constructed, becoming absorbed in it as if to make the ego its guardian and law."

With this myopic view, the ego rarely sees beyond itself. Generally, the activities and drives of this ego-based personality do not allow for the stillness in which we can hear the call of the vastly subtler self. That other self, our soul nature, is ever in residence as we live in our physical-material reality. This self is hidden by the noise and drives of the world and our lack of attention to its existence.

Our Developmental Stages

Our entry into the material world as infants is driven foremost by the survival instinct. From this beginning, the infant embarks on a journey of growing and expressing increased mastery of its biology. The developmental progression from birth at a physical and psychological level has definite patterns and transitions. Certain milestones of development that are age specific must occur if there is to be a normal physical and psychological growth and maturation.

Renowned psychoanalyst, Erik Erikson, addressed specifically the developmental stages and the areas of attempted psychological mastery that must occur in those specific stages. Piaget's classic work on children also shows us stages of child development using copious research, observation,

> *What really has to (go) is our false self created by our own mind, ego, and culture. It is a pretense, a bogus identity, a passing fad, a psychological construct that gets in the way of who we are and always were.... This is the objective and metaphysical True Self.*
>
> RICHARD ROHR

Aligning Your Dual Natures: The Limited Self and the Eternal Self

and journey metaphors; he reveals this development through the eyes of the child, providing a clear view of the Limited Self's necessary dominance in young human consciousness.

If a child grows with the proper guidance, developmental stages occur in proper sequence. These stages, however, are influenced by the interaction of parents, significant others, and the community in which the child lives. Through words, example and behaviors powerful messages are delivered to the child: these contribute to his own self-identification. The child receives both overt and covert messages that have enormous potential for interpretation, and thus add to the intrigue and complexity of the youth's emotional and psychological journey.

The Limited Self is naturally rooted in this journey involving the physiological wiring of our nature in a physical world. By necessity, the child focuses on gaining greater skill over specific need areas, body mastery, and physical navigation in the world. This leads to body-based self-identification.

No wonder our self-esteem is reinforced by the idea that external mastery in the physical world is a natural source of happiness. So many messages in society reinforce this. Athletes become heroes; fashion models are idolized. Popularity is often based on glamour, wealth, and personality. Is it any wonder the young psyche can become confused?

The absorption and interpretation of messages, impressions, and ideas create an experience of self-identity. There are not only layers upon layers of experience, but also enmeshed layers of subtle reinforcement, and the co-mingling of these layers that create the masquerade of our "real self."

> *The ego feeling we are aware of now is…only a shrunken vestige of a far more extensive feeling – a feeling which embraced the universe and expressed an inseparable connection of the ego with the external world.*
>
> SIGMUND FREUD

With the increasing capacity to contemplate, examine and verbalize one's experiences, the child feels that what we are calling the Limited Self is actually the core reality of his essence. Since the Limited Self must, of necessity, be identified with its biological journey and the physical, material world, it strives to access the world from this early core identification. The child seeks its happiness from the senses and the material world. Although the progressive formation of this Limited Self results in an undeniably real self, we are in truth, something vastly more complex, more wondrous.

Though most individuals abandon the ideas and desires of youth by changing or modifying them with experience, yet we still claim this Limited Self as solid and enduring even though the frailty of that perception can be seen in the reflecting mirror of changing experiences. One of the great delusive ideas posits the solidity and permanence of the Limited Self amidst impermanence and fragmentation.

The more we bring these distorted, fragmented areas to conscious awareness, the greater will be the possibility of integrating them. The greater the denial about opposing parts within us, the greater the potential that we will experience conflict and lack personal integration. Denial and lack of self-knowledge perpetuate fragmentation and lessen our chances of experiencing continuous fulfillment and happiness.

Illusory Happiness

When asked to write down what we feel would give us happiness, many of us will naturally respond with answers centered on physical-material objects, or success in that realm. Some will look to relationships or about love more generally for happiness. Some may believe that the possession of, or the constant access to another person is the source of our happiness. This is because the Limited Self does not fully understand that the desire to experience love is also an invitation to know more of the Eternal Self. So instead, we interpret love as a sensory or material experience associated with its own nature.

Happiness for the Limited Self has to be tied to the experiences or desires of life in a physical body in a material world. In this state of being, our capacity for happiness is not only determined by our habitual state of mind, whether positive or negative, but by our emotional response to events. Emotions become charged with expectation and interpretation. This generally leads to replaying and reinterpreting along similar ideas or themes. We replay memories and interpret them yet again. And off we go on a repetitive cycle that is difficult to break. Let's take a deeper look at how such thought patterns work.

How Habit Patterns are Formed

Our interpretations of events create energy. This blueprint energy creates grooves in our brains that allow for further movement of energy through which our consciousness travels. New experiences tend to gravitate into existing energy grooves. Once a particular thought groove is activated by a repetitive thought, a tendency is formed. It is extremely difficult to change the tendencies of the physical mind for so many of our thoughts are automatic and therefore unconscious.

In the last few decades, scientists have shown that we can change the structure and function of our brains by the way we think. This newly conceptualized feature of the brain is called neuroplasticity. For years, the conventional wisdom of neuroscience held that the hardware

> *DNA is controlled by extra-cellular signals, including the energetic messages emanating from our positive and negative thoughts. By retraining our minds to create healthy beliefs, we can change the physiology of our trillion-celled bodies. Dr. Lipton's profoundly hopeful synthesis of the latest and best research in cell biology and quantum physics is being hailed as a major breakthrough in our awareness of how our cells, our bodies and our minds work.*
>
> BRUCE LIPTON,
> *Biology of Belief*

of the brain is fixed and immutable—that we are stuck with what we were born with. Yet *Wall Street Journal* science writer, Sharon Begley, reveals an entirely new paradigm in her book, *Train the Mind, Change the Brain*. She describes pioneering experiments in the field of neuroplasticity that investigate how the brain can undergo wholesale change. These experiments reveal that the brain is capable not only of altering its structure but also of generating new neurons, even into old age.

By the act of mental repetition, and the mental replay of ideas, we create new energy grooves. Our power to create new energy grooves means we have the power to recreate, re-imagine, and re-energize any event that occurred in the physical-material world.

You stand at a crossroads with every experience in life from smelling a flower to failing an exam at school, dealing with a promotion to falling in love or coping with a major loss. How you interpret the experience determines your reality and sets up the blueprint for similar experiences in the future. Your interpretive capacity crystallizes these perceptions in a manner that either integrates or fragments your self, creating harmony or dissonance. The repetition of these ideas forges self-identity and creates energy grooves and memory grooves in the physiology of the brain itself.

The repetition of these themes can lead to either positive or negative self-talk. The more you energize and repeat any theme, the greater and deeper are the energy grooves available for that theme. And the deeper and more pronounced the energy groove, the more likely that you will repeat the same interpretations. The late self-help author Robert Collier put it this way: "One comes to believe whatever one repeats to oneself sufficiently often, whether the statement be true or false. It comes to be the dominating thought in one's mind." It is imperative, therefore, that you become more aware of your habitual trends of thought.

Confusion can result when you place too much emphasis on your interpretations of events, experiences and interactions. These interpretations are simply the movement of energy in chemical, biological and energy fields. They are not the true reflectors of reality. The habit of repeating ideas may help you feel solid. You may mistake that "solidity" for who you truly are. Ultimately, that is an illusion. You are more than your biology, interpretations, emotions, and habits of thought!

Psychology and Self-Help

Most self-help books are based on the premise that to achieve happiness or peace, we must better understand and master our psychological underpinnings.

But it is *only* the Limited Self that can achieve greater self-understanding through psychological approaches to self-discovery. This is a worthy endeavor, of course, for introspection, self-examination, and self-analysis are helpful tools in the process of knowing ourselves. Psychology is about the journey of consciousness, addressing as well the physiological aspects of life and their impact on consciousness. But if the consciousness of the Limited Self becomes the only area of investigation, the discovery of a larger, spiritual Self will be sacrificed and with it, the attainment of true integration.

You need to find the middle path. Bypassing the Limited Self in your efforts to access your spiritual self will not bring freedom and happiness anymore than the reverse. Buried, denied and unresolved psychological issues will continue to fester and do damage if left unaddressed. Without deep inner work, those issues remain and will spring up as you move past the Limited Self to delve more deeply into your spiritual nature. John Welwood speaks to this in his *Toward a Psychology of Awakening:* "As awareness starts to move beyond the boundaries of the conditioned personality structure, this expansion inevitably challenges that structure, flushing out old, subconscious, reactive patterns that often emerge with a vengeance."

When these reactive patterns are flushed to the surface, psychology can be a helpful therapeutic tool. Psychological assistance from the hands of trained professionals can give you an invaluable gift, the gift of greater self knowledge and the possibility of understanding more of yourself, your journey, and the movement of your own consciousness. However, psychology in general has little value in the territory and the analysis of the spiritual nature of man. Any lasting transformation of your human consciousness ultimately has to provide the unshakable realization that you are at your core, a spiritual being, possessing an unchangeable nature rooted in joy.

Introducing the Eternal Self

Beyond the Limited Self is another Self, constant, changeless, integrated, unbounded by physiology, unaffected by alternating psychological states, impervious to societal or cultural influences. It functions by intuition, free of interpretation and faulty self-definition.

This Eternal Self is not searching for happiness because it already exists in the state of unalterable joy intrinsic to our very being. Your drive for happiness is not simply the thrust of your desire for self-gratification or for pleasure at a biological level. Rather, it is the spiritual call to a vision of yourself that is often obscured by the seeming reality of the material world.

What if, in the search to discover who you are, you should find this expansive, radiant self underneath the layers of personality and material identifications? How would you experience it? Many of the world's spiritual traditions describe this self as the essence of Spirit, manifesting in creation through the vibratory energy of love and light. Though you may not consciously be aware of this self, it is nevertheless real and truly who you are. While you experience life as a physical being, this self remains profoundly separate, yet powerfully a part of you, immutable, unchangeable, enduring, permanent. This self is the expression of your soul nature. Here is a poem I wrote about this essential Self.

Forever More I Shall Be

I am
I am that which is
I am that which will always be.

I am immutable
I am the fortress
I am beyond all destruction.

I am deathless
I withstand all
For I am all.

When the world and the universe of matter
Shall crumble, I shall remain serene!
When the sun shall fall from the heavens
My light shall light the world of worlds!

When I shed forevermore my forms
I shall be with form
And yet formless!

For I am
And forever more I shall be!

The Eternal Self is Spirit participating in the journey of being human. If this is so, how, then, might we find greater happiness, especially if the essence of our being is already joy itself? Perhaps this joy is undiscovered, perhaps this peace is uncultivated, but nevertheless, in the purest sense, that eternal joy exists. And so the art of finding true happiness lies in accessing and empowering who we

> *Being is not only beyond but also deep within every form as its innermost invisible and indestructible essence. This means that it is accessible to you now as your own deepest self, your true nature….You can know it only when the mind is still. When you are present, when your attention is fully and intensely in the Now.*
>
> ECKART TOLLE

truly are, spiritual beings who are living a physical-material journey. Without the journey inward, we may find that lasting happiness is always just beyond our grasp. *This journey requires deep commitment to self-discovery, and steadfast patience, as the Irish saying goes, the "patience that can conquer destiny."*

The Well of Silence Within

Meditation has been used through the centuries as a method for acquiring spiritual self-knowledge. It is based on the idea that as the consciousness becomes interiorized, we have more access to our essence or true nature. "Be still and know that I am God" conveys this truth with simple clarity. The silence of meditation is not just a passive quietness. It embodies a dynamic and vast consciousness far beyond our usual experience. In this mental stillness, we can access our own hidden consciousness.

Real empowerment must include the cultivation of a relationship with your truest self, the Eternal Self, which rests in the center of your being. This Self begins to emerge when you peel away the layers of ego consciousness through meditation, introspection and other awareness-based practices. All beings, no matter how reactionary, fearful, violent or lost, can open themselves to the sacred within and become free. Spirit is your very being. Meditation allows you access to the deeper regions of your spiritual nature, connects you with the Divine presence within, and will provide you with a clearer vision of the truth. Scheduling time each day for meditation practice is essential not only for your peace and well being and empowerment, but also for experiencing your Eternal Self, the true source of lasting happiness. There are countless meditation techniques available and myriad philosophies about the proper method of meditation. Finding an effective and suitable style of meditation can take time and experimentation but will prove invaluable. One technique is offered below.

Meditation Technique

The proper posture for meditation is very important.

- Sitting in a straight back chair is recommended.
- The feet should be flat on the floor, pointed straight ahead.
- In a state of relaxation, maintain a straight spine, to the best of your ability without strain or discomfort.
- Place your hands, with palms turned gently upward, near the junction between your legs and thighs. (Note: Meditation techniques, in general, should not be practiced in a position where the individual is lying down in a bed. When lying down, the meditative state too easily becomes a sleep state. If an individual has the physical ability to sit either in a chair with feet flat on the floor—or cross-legged on the floor on a flat surface—the sitting posture should be assumed. In general avoid sitting on a bed, for consciousness usually associates the bed with sleep.)

This meditation technique involves focusing your attention at the point between the eyebrows known as the "spiritual eye." This is a center that increases our spiritual connectedness as we focus upon it. If you are having difficulty in achieving or maintaining the proper eye position for your meditation, the following suggestion may assist you in getting the correct angle for your focus gaze. The eyes should be turned gently and slightly upward.

Pencil Technique for Proper Gaze

Visualize holding a #2 pencil eraser at the spiritual eye. Visualize the eraser resting on the forehead between and slightly above the eyebrows, with the pencil parallel to the ground. Allow your focus to move to where you visualize the point of the pencil to be. Keep the gaze focused at that spot. This technique is not part of the practice itself, but will prevent you from placing excessive strain on the eyes and help develop a better habit pattern for meditation.

Note: There should be no strain or tension. This is a natural, pleasant position for the eyes. If there is strain or tension, the gaze may be turned too far upward, or the eyes may be slightly crossed. Check the eye position.

Preparation for Meditation:

- Visualize that you are encircled by white light that either outlines the body or appears as a spherical egg-shape. It is the <u>intention</u> to place white light around the body that summons a greater connection with Spirit and strengthens the energy field.

- After visualizing the white light in this way, begin to observe the breath in a relaxed state of mind. Maintain the correct posture with spine erect and feet flat on the floor.

- Affirm that the surrounding white light of Spirit divinely protects you. (Example: "I am surrounded by the light field of the Divine. I am ever protected. I am ever embraced by the Divine Force.") Repeat this protection affirmation, or a similar one, five or six times.

- Now, in this relaxed state of mind, begin to observe the breath without any attempt to regulate it. Neither speed up nor slow down the rhythm of the breath. Simply observe the inhalation and exhalation as it naturally flows in and out.

- See yourself as "piggy-backing" on each inhalation and exhalation. Mentally say, "I ride the inward breath." As you naturally begin to exhale, mentally say, "I ride the outward breath." Continue this pattern for approximately 15 minutes. Visualize yourself riding the inward breath and the outward breath. Then change the repetition of words on the inhaling and exhaling breath to "I am That[1]".

Additional affirmations that may be mentally repeated prior to or following the use of this meditation technique:

I ride the inward breath.
I ride the outward breath.
I am one with that breath.
Reveal Thyself.

Note: Effective meditation techniques are available from Self-Realization Fellowship in the form of lessons that are delivered to your home every two weeks.

For information contact:

Self-Realization Fellowship
3880 San Rafael Drive
Los Angeles, CA 90065-3219
323-225-2471
http//www.yogananda-srf.org

Such techniques of will-charged visualization and spiritualized affirmation are also powerful conduits and conveyors of truth that promote access to this highest self. The irony is that our spiritual, expansive, all-knowing self is never in pursuit of its own happiness. Its nature is already joy, peace, and bliss. In its silence, the Eternal Self is

---

[1] "I am That" refers to our being One with the Indwelling Spirit.

summoning the Limited Self into a greater alignment with itself. In the Greek myth, Narcissus falls in love with his own image reflected in a still pool of water. In a spiritual interpretation, he may be seeing the truth of his own divine nature reflecting back in the still waters.

While this reflection is generally obscured, there is nevertheless a powerful drive within us not only to perceive our true image, our true Self, but to become fully one with it. We desire the joy that is more than an extension of the happiness of the earth. Seemingly just out of reach, we tend to fall back on our belief in the tangible self of change and vacillating, unstable circumstances. We may operate on the myth that this kaleidoscope of images is our true self and that if we can run fast enough, we will catch and possess ourselves and achieve a state of unchanging happiness. Like the proverbial dog chasing its own tail, we go round and round in search of something that is already within us.

True access lies in the stillness and the subtleties of the movement of Spirit. Eckart Tolle wrote: "Your innermost sense of self, of who you are, is inseparable from stillness. This is the I Am that is deeper than name and form." His words are an invitation to you to embark on a voyage of self-discovery. They invite your activity-driven mind and sense identification to move past the pursuits of the world, toward calmness, serenity, peace, tranquility, and self-knowing beyond any definition. This is where deep meditation will take you.

If you believe that in time you will possess happiness because of the nature of your dreams and goals, the world offers strong encouragement to continue to pursue that pathway. Perhaps nothing that others say will alter the momentum of that journey. But if you doubt that the world in and of itself will be able to provide happiness, know that doubt itself can be a catalyst for you to go deeper, thus creating a bridge to a new level of integration between the two selves.

The tools of meditation, visualization and affirmation are the bridge-builders for the fragmented parts of our Limited Self. To achieve true, lasting happiness, the self of the world must come into alliance, alignment and attunement with the Divine aspect of the self.

Characteristics of the Limited Self and Eternal Self

Limited Self	Eternal Self
Ego-driven consciousness	Spirit-based consciousness
Identifies with the body and the material world	Not subject to identification with body, senses or material pleasures
Biological and psychological identification is foundational	Spirit in man beyond all definition and identification
Shaped by experiences and interpretations of those experiences	Immutable, absolute in Being regardless of experiences
Resides in our genetic heritage	Independent of genetic heritage
Desires to seek and possess happiness	Never in pursuit of its own happiness; continually joyful
Progresses through an innate developmental pattern of psychological and biological stages	Manifests in creation through the vibratory energy of love and light
Impacted and changed by circumstances and faulty self-definition	Not impacted by changing conditions or circumstances
Struggles with feelings of powerlessness against the Law of Change	Changeless nature is constant joy, peace, bliss
Ever changing and unstable due to circumstances, with illusion of control	Has enduring permanence, unfaltering truth, vibratory consistency with spirit
Happiness associated with fulfillment of biological drives and gratification	Happiness inherent in being independent of external desires

Affirmations to Help Integrate Your Dual Nature

For Integration
Attuned, Aligned,
Integrated Self
Content in Being,
Peaceful in Serenity,
Awake in Spirit.

For Joy-filled Bliss
Being in knowing
I am.
Joy-filled,
light-illuminated,
ever penetrated,
ever known.
Joy-filled bliss I am.
Joy-filled bliss I am.

For Becoming One with the Light
I am the Light
of all suns.
I possess the power
of all creations.
My name is the name
of all Light,
all suns,
all power,
and all creations.

For Seeing My Face in God
I behold the face of God.
I parted the curtains of penetration
and the face I saw
was my own.

For Becoming One with All That Is
In becoming one
with nature
I claim my
nature.
I am Spirit
in nature.

For Silent Discovery
In silence,
the seeker finds
himself.

For Intentional Focus
Intentioned focus increases my power
of concentration.
In concentration
I perceive the whole,
and the parts,
moving in perfected
harmony.

For Greater Purified Consciousness
Oh Lord, may I become less of myself
in ego-based consciousness
that I may become ever more one with Thee.
May I become truly a purified conduit
of Your love, of Your light, of Your grace.

For Becoming a Mirror of the Divine
May I become a perfected mirror
of the divine essence
which is You, Oh Lord.

Tree with Pink and White Blossoms
By Yvonne G. Christenson

CHAPTER 2

Stepping Stones to Change

A journey of a thousand miles begins with a single step…
You are invited to take that first step.

The Journey Within

Anything truly worthwhile requires effort, consistency, and fortitude. The journey to true, lasting happiness is no different. Becoming more self-aware is a life-long pursuit well worth the effort because by learning to live life more consciously, we do change. The person we once were transforms. Deeply rooted patterns are dissolved and new life-enhancing habits are created. *"Every wakeful step, every mindful act is the direct path to awakening"* said the Buddha.

This journey requires the greatest resilience, however. To penetrate deeply into your inner nature, you must be willing to fully see and understand areas that have been hidden, difficult, or have held you back from your true potential.

The Eight Stepping Stones are practical, systematic and effective techniques to help you change. That is why practicing the process of foundational change begins now. Beginning the process now *while* you are reading about other concepts and principles will offer a transfusion of energy, excitement and encouragement to help you feel emboldened and confident about your personal journey. You, like all of us, are a creator. Like any artist working with soft clay, you can mold your life into a new sculpture of possibilities. You are capable of expressing more joy than you thought possible. As you become more unified in your own unique expression, your two selves align in the most beneficial way.

The complexity of your two selves—Limited and Eternal—presents you, however, with the formidable task of attempting to transform your self-concept from human to divine. Your spiritual nature is entwined with body senses and the alluring material nature of the world. Yet, Spirit expresses Itself independent of your lower nature. Since your two selves may lack a shared experience of meaning, coordination, dialogue, communication, and integration, you may experience difficulties in attempting to know yourself and determine what will truly give you happiness. The Stepping Stones will assist you with this integration.

Perhaps you feel overwhelmed by the process of integrating the two selves. Where do you start? How will we recognize those parts of ourselves needing integration and healing? How will you know you are successful? Breaking this process down into manageable parts is essential. You need to be able to measure results and set specific goals. The Stepping Stone process, clearly outlined below, will help you do that.

The Eight Stepping Stones to Change

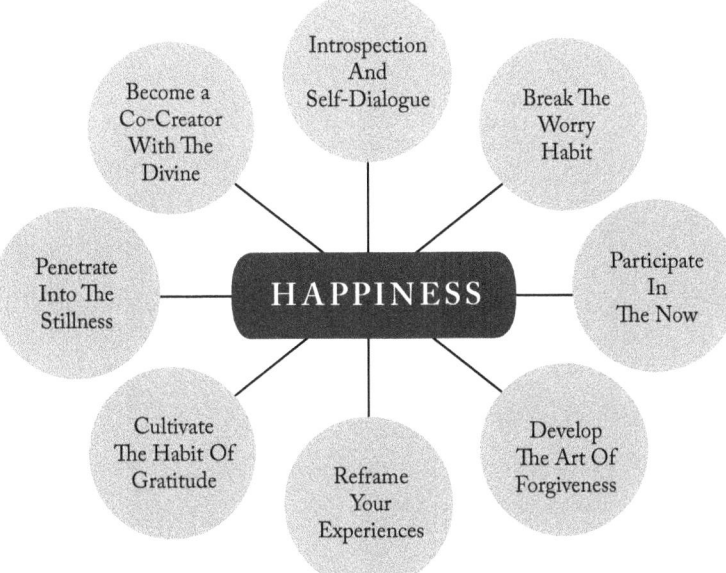

1. Introspection and self-dialogue. (Increase self-awareness)
2. Break the "worry habit." (Liberate consciousness)
3. Participate in the Now. (Be more present)
4. Develop the "Art of Forgiveness." (Free yourself from the perception and effects of old injuries)
5. Reframe your experiences. ("Reframe and Claim" by the art of new definition)
6. Cultivate the habit of gratitude. (Gratefulness is a spiritual magnet that increases the flow of the good)
7. Accept and penetrate into the stillness. (Well-balanced and effective meditation techniques)
8. Become a co-creator with the Divine. (Greater alignment of the two selves with a deeper penetration into the Eternal Self)

Each Stepping Stone to Change will be your focus for a three-week period. In these sequences, habit patterns will begin to energetically and physiologically change your moldable and changeable brain; repetitions of the new rituals and ways of thinking will actually create new energy grooves. Repetition deepens the capacity for reflective thought. Negative habit patterns are not uprooted by brief musings or a statement or two. At an energetic level and physical level, new channels of thought must be created through practice. In addition to repetition, increased discipline will be acquired. Acquiring discipline helps train will power. Will power is then further fueled by dynamic will. The addition of spiritualized affirmations further activates the dynamic thrust of change. And this dynamic will be intensified if you use a thought-for-the-day paired with a spiritualized affirmation.

Each of the Stepping Stones discussed in this chapter includes introspection questions, as well as material you are to repeat every day for three weeks in order to establish habit patterns that reading and inspiration alone cannot create. Repetition accelerates foundational change. By revolving new positive thoughts in your mind, you will actually create those new energy grooves in your brain. During each Step of this process your day should include:

- journaling for fifteen minutes.
- a spiritualized affirmation.
- a thought for the day.
- exercises for that Step.

Write your chosen affirmation for that Step on three, three-by-five file cards. Place those cards over your desk, on your bathroom mirror, above the kitchen sink, on your car dashboard—wherever you are most likely to see the card and thus be reminded to say the affirmation again. You may speak it out loud or mentally, depending upon circumstances. Aim for fifteen repetitions each day. This daily practice is the heart of the workbook to systematically begin to create change.

Affirmations Defined

Before we move on to describe the first Stepping Stone, I want to be certain that you understand what affirmations are and how they can power charge your life. In every day speech, we may use the word "affirm" simply to denote "yes" or to make a larger positive assertion of one's ideas or one's self. Most use the word as described in Webster's dictionary — "1: confirm 2: to assert positively 3: to make a solemn and formal declaration or assertion in place of an oath."

Affirmation as used here, however, applies to a specific technique, based on spiritual and scientific principles, that allows for a heightened level of alignment of your consciousness with Spirit. This alignment allows you to tap into the very force of creation and claim your true nature. By stating an affirmation, you can claim your nature in words and then these energized words penetrate and expand into deeper recesses of self-knowledge. Affirmations used properly have the power to activate more of your spiritual power. Through the faithful and correct practice of affirmations, you can align yourself to the truth of your own spiritual nature. An affirmation creates a spiritualized force field expressed in words, with energy, movement and momentum.

Affirmations thus start a potent vibration, which corresponds to both a specific energy frequency and a state of consciousness in seed form. Over time, the affirmation begins to override other smaller vibrations, which eventually become absorbed by the affirmation. Affirmations become power charged by your focused attention and application of will-based energy.

Key Concepts about Affirmations

Affirmations are an effective technique for change if you desire to:

- Change circumstances in your life to more positive ones.
- Unleash your creative power by the dynamic force of intention.
- Create new possibilities in your life.
- Explore new talents and new dimensions of yourself.
- Strengthen the power of your imagination and visualizations.
- Stop negative self-talk.
- Uproot tenacious negative thinking that limit your happiness.
- Deepen spiritual life by exploring and expanding consciousness.

Principles Behind Affirmations

- They assist in creating new possibilities in any part of your life.
- They deepen the energy blueprint in creation and stir movement toward manifestation of the desired outcome.
- They increase your ability to develop willpower and discipline.
- Energy seeks its vibrational counterpart, and so affirmations seek manifestation through magnetic attraction or repulsion.
- They improve your conditions and circumstances, as you <u>affirm and visualize</u> changed circumstances. Affirmations thus become charged with your <u>activated will</u>.
- Creation manifests through this dynamic process, for the power of creation resides in your innate nature.

Change Your Thoughts, Change Your Life

As you change your thoughts, you change your energy. As you change your energy, that which is attracted to you changes.

That truth is spiritual law in operation. No matter what your conditions, you have the power to redefine them. No matter what your situation, you have the power to visualize something different and something new. No matter what your circumstances, your power to co-create with the universe is amplified by your engagement with it. You are a potent co-creator of Divine possibilities and discoveries. Your nature, as energized love and light, is in search of the highest vibration of itself.

Affirmations are a true and valid tool of consciousness transformation. Their power resides not only in their positive impact on the Limited Self, that part of us existing in a material world subject to decay and death; affirmations also allow for greater self-integration. This creates a bridge between our diverging selves—Limited and Eternal— thus promoting alignment, coordination, attunement, and harmonious cooperation between them.

Affirmations also alter energy and thought patterns. Your habitual attitudes form neural circuits in the brain. By choosing different habitual thoughts, you may rewire the brain, creating new pathways to form new attitudes about yourself or your relationships. Affirmations can be may be made more powerful by:

1. Frequency of repetition.
2. Regularity of repetition.
3. Clarity in wording, consistent with physical and spiritual law.
4. Maintaining consistency in the wording of the affirmation.
5. Physical relaxing during affirmation practice.

When using affirmations, repeat the same basic idea, or content for an extended period of time. You dilute their power by continuously rewording, reworking, or changing themes. Additionally, relaxation during affirmation practice deepens the access to the subconscious mind and to the spiritual stream of divine consciousness.

The Importance of Conscious Language in Affirmations

Any affirmation that is preceded with the words, "I Am" makes a spiritual statement. "I Am" refers directly to the name of God, who is beyond all names. "I Am the I Am" may be thought of as a name of God. When you say, "I Am" anything, you are stating that the God within you is in that circumstance or situation. The use of the words "I Am" in affirmation should be clearly stated with the proper spiritual intention, harmonized with spiritual truth.

The affirmation, "I am wealthy and prosperous" is a very different affirmation from this one: "Money and wealth are mine." When there is a statement, "I Am" it is a statement of the God-aspect in man, a vibration with man in creation and man in manifestation. Instead of stating, "A new house is manifesting for me," affirm: "I am one with the Eternal Source of all creation. I am one with the abundant supply of that Divine force that is ever-creating abundance and prosperity in my life Now." (This affirmation could be separated into two parts if desired.) When the affirmation is so stated, it recognizes the Eternal Source, the highest source of creation, the Divine Source of all life. By recognizing that Source you draw closer to alignment with It, synchronizing the vibratory energy that is within you and outside you in creation.

You would do well not to limit your idea of prosperity or any other theme to one or more specific items. For example, to believe that you are prosperous based on the sudden appearance of a new house limits you and improperly measures the stream of possibilities. Take care not to limit your concept of what might flow from the Divine Source itself.

{ *Thoughts are things* EDGAR CAYCE }

The Spiritual Source is the supplier of all. Affirmations that directly, or indirectly, affirm that truth generate access to the Source itself. To believe your possibilities are limited in any way, is to negate the truth of your being a receiver from the Eternal well-spring of all-giving, all-supply, and all-life. In the statement *"Money and wealth are mine,"* wealth again is seen as the source of the manifestation. That affirmation does not recognize the opportunity for co-creation with Spirit. The ego-identified man becomes the primary focus. Properly formulated affirmations acknowledge that wealth is a manifestation or by-product, of that Eternal Source. As you deepen your practice of affirmation, you may become aware of certain contrary beliefs. If you affirm greater creativity, but your self-dialogue and interior thought process associate creativity with financial need, then your results will be diminished. Any thought that implies "creativity cannot generate financial success" minimizes the possibility of success through creative and artistic work. Creativity paired with the idea of insufficiency will always, by the law of magnetic attraction, create a state of lack. Despite such a belief, you should affirm that prosperity and creativity may be powerfully paired. Over time, your affirmation will help you achieve creative expression and financial success simultaneously. This applies to all themes that charge your affirmations as you embark upon the Stepping Stones to Transformation that follow.

Stepping Stone #1
Introspection and
Self-Dialogue/ Journaling

"As a Man Thinketh in his heart, so is he." Proverbs

The great Wisdom Traditions remind us that we are the creators of our destiny. Our ability to create begins with right thinking, which we can hear in the words we say to ourselves continually throughout the day. We are the architects of our own lives. Every thought we think creates that very reality for us, significantly impacting everything in life, from our relationships, to our finances, our dreams, health and well-being. It is imperative, therefore, for you to discover just what your beliefs are if you are to create the life you wish to live.

Journaling is a highly effective tool in this process. Through it you can learn to become aware of the thought patterns you are creating, often unconsciously. By journaling, you can view your experiences more objectively, in a way that enables you to discern how you actually view and live your life. Journaling is a form of introspection, a way of uncovering the truth within, and thus, a vital practice to increase self-awareness. You cannot change things you do not see or know. It is crucial, then, to increase your knowing.

Journaling is best practiced for a minimum of 15 minutes a day, preferably early in the day, after a period of reflection (such as meditation or affirmations), if possible. Journaling will make you more present in your own personal journey and increase your ability to self-dialogue. *The Artist's Way* by Julia Cameron has an excellent section called *Morning Pages* about journaling and its relationship to creativity. She describes how it is possible to uncover a deeper self-understanding: *"…. the pages are a pathway to a strong sense and clear sense of self. They are a trail that we follow into our own interior… Anyone who faithfully writes morning pages will be led to a connection with a source of wisdom within."(31)*. Focused questions can make journaling even more potent; such questions and exercises accompany each stepping stone.

Analyze and Affirm Your Positive Qualities

To begin, reflect on the personal qualities that have contributed positively to your life and relationships. Write these down. They may be as simple as "I listen well to my friends;" "I take care of my health" or "I tend to bounce back quickly after a setback." Then analyze and write down which behavior patterns deter you from finding positive solutions and good communication and connections in your relationships.

Now write down affirmations that state only positive qualities and outcomes in the areas you desire to improve. If you tend to feel insecure, you might say, for instance, "I am strong, secure, loved and protected." If you worry constantly about money, you might say "I have abundant resources with which to live a full life." Use only those affirmations that express the potency of the positive attributes and awareness, and suggest the spiritual attunement that you feel you desire to achieve.

These affirmations radically train the mind's ability to perceive differently. You will become changed by that which you affirm because you attract a higher vibratory energy level, resonant with Spirit, that can expand your true awareness of yourself and erase the shadows of past deeds, mistakes, and misunderstandings.

As you proceed in this process you will become more aware of your shortcomings as well as your strengths. Remember that becoming aware is the first step toward transforming any unwanted tendencies. Ultimately, it doesn't matter what negative traits have hounded you in the past. You can alter the course of your life through will-directed thoughts and words in the form of spiritual affirmations.

A growing body of scientific evidence supports the theory that your thoughts influence your life dramatically. The Princeton Engineering

Anomalies Research Program (PEAR) has been compiling evidence for more than twenty-seven years showing how the human mind influences what it focuses on. It is a fascinating study, with thousands of documented experiments. Beyond its revolutionary technological applications and scientific impact, the evidence of an active role of consciousness in establishing physical reality has profound implications for our view of ourselves, our relationships to others, and the cosmos in which we exist.

Introspection Technique: *Name Your Themes*

The greater your ability to self-reflect, the more effective will be your practice of journaling and your use of affirmations.

Write on a piece of paper five main themes that you mentally revisit most often. Reflect on why you feel these themes recur. To help deepen your understanding, think about the challenges you've had in life as well as the dreams and goals you have not yet fulfilled. Include your feelings about these challenges, goals and dreams and why you believe they've become a part of your life.

For example, perhaps you have always struggled to make ends meet. Ask yourself why you think you haven't achieved greater abundance. You may answer, "People have to work a nine-to-five job and get paid what they give you. Life isn't about fun." Where did this or a similar belief come from? Did you hear a parent say it over and over again when you were a teen or maybe it was your distant relative who struggled through the Great Depression and never quite got over it?

You may discover certain themes about relationships, intimacy, education, career, or other areas of life. Whatever they may be, write them down in your journal, along with what you feel you have learned from these experiences. How have they contributed to a greater level of self-understanding?

As you look deeper, you may recognize certain patterns over many years that have negatively affected your health, relationships or financial well-being. Sometimes you may repeat various themes because of a subconscious sense of guilt, blaming yourself as an act of spiritual atonement for what has occurred. For example, perhaps you made a mistake in the past that deprived you of an important educational, financial or relationship goal. Perhaps you now tend to stay more distant, uninvolved, uncommitted in that area of life out of an unconscious desire to avoid repeating the same mistake. You may never have processed that experience and may feel bad about yourself, feeling you have failed and thus don't "deserve" success in the present.

In what ways might this tendency apply to your circumstances and the themes that you mentally repeat?

Introspection Opportunity

Now let's take this introspective approach deeper. Write down the answers to the following questions. Rate yourself on a scale of 1-5, 5 being the highest positive number.

- Do you enjoy participating with others in close emotional connection?
- Does emotional intimacy feel comfortable? If not, in what ways?
- Do you ever feel you are mimicking intimacy rather than participating in it?
- If you have encountered significant loss or a tragedy, can any aspect of that negative experience be used in assisting another person, or group of people?
- Out of suffering, have you found any way to contribute to another or others? How has your experience changed you?

- Do you have the ability to listen and really hear the thoughts of others?

- Do you practice reflecting back what you believe people are saying to you before proceeding mentally or in conversation?

- Do you need to improve upon that capacity?

- Do you see yourself as having a capacity and willingness to share?

- Do you begrudge having to give to another and feel that it takes away from yourself?

- Do you see yourself as having sympathy and empathy for the suffering of another?

- Has there been any loss in your life that you feel increased your opportunity to be more present in the now?

Honest self-inquiry, such as that outlined above, is a key Stepping Stone on your journey toward deliberate happiness. Journaling and introspection should become a natural part of your life, assisting you to deepen self-awareness in order to find sources of inner strength and mastery.

Now practice the ritual of Step #1 every day for three weeks:

- **Journaling for 15 minutes on Self-Dialogue.**
- **Positive introspection on this theme.**
- **Affirmations for the First Step:**

*Celestial sun
molten force of power
enter into me.
The power of the light
does change me.*

Or

*Celestial sun
radiate through me.
The fields of light
do change me.*

Pair your affirmation with a thought such as this one from the Sufi poet Rumi:

*The way of love is not a subtle argument.
The door there is devastation.
Birds make great sky-circles of their freedom.
How do they learn it? They fall, and falling, they're given wings.*

Stepping Stone # 2
Break the Worry Habit

Analyze and break the debilitating and circular nature of worry.

Worry provides an excellent window through which to see areas of your psyche that need the greatest infusion of faith, positive thinking and reinforcement. Do you continually worry about money, love, health? If you remain unaware of this tendency, the worry habit may go on endlessly, playing and replaying the same old themes throughout your life.

What is worry? Webster defines it as "mental distress or agitation resulting from concern, usually for something impending or anticipated." We have all no doubt experienced worry over something. We have found ourselves in its grip when the mind fixates on possible negative consequences. These consequences are based on ideas that essentially state, "what *if* this happens?" Worry calls on the power of imagination and visualization, but its nature is circular and destructive. It is not the imagination of positive creation, stretching out in creative potential.

Worry is anxiety-producing. When you examine your thought processes, you may be astonished at the amount of time and energy that is used up this way. Worry is not active problem-solving. It cannot change any circumstances. It is therefore limiting, constricting, energy draining, and stifles creative thought.

Ultimately, worry is tension. On some level of your being you are not relaxed, accepting, living in the present moment. Perhaps you are attempting to defend, or brace yourself from the worst possible imagined outcome, rather than being available to the fullness of life, in whatever shape or form it arrives.

The irony about worry is how little of what we worry about actually comes to pass. Ralph Waldo Emerson wisely put it this way:

Some of your hurts you have cured,
and the sharpest you still have survived,
but what torments of grief you endured
from the evil which never arrived.

Worry is indeed a torment and worthy of every effort to eradicate! None of us wishes to live in endless cycles of worry that zap our energy and deplete us emotionally. Our lives only have so much energy available. We need to pay attention to worry because the energy of imagination used in visualizing negative outcomes has a powerful influence. The mind is an amazing tool. Focusing on something continuously provides energy to that thought and gives it texture and form in physical reality. Worry eclipses positive possibilities. Negative energy which anticipates negative outcomes can impact the physical body. The body rallies as if it is in a place of crisis or emergency, over-taxing the adrenals and the entire endocrine system. Worry tells the body to respond by fight or flight, while the only real danger is the mental replaying of ideas in the imagination.

According to acclaimed endocrinologist Hans Seyle, author of *The Stress of Life*, worry and stress proceed in three stages which he categorizes as the Alarm, the Resistance, and the Exhaustion phases. Prolonged stress and worry produce in the final stage, "psychosomatic diseases, emotional breakdown, adrenal exhaustion, insomnia, heart & blood pressure complications, and host of other very painful symptoms associated with burnout. In summary:

1. Worry locks thought processes into negative streams of habit.
2. Worry blocks creative flow. It stifles imagination and the release of imagination in a positive flow of mental thought.

3. Worry restricts our access to Spirit. It ties us increasingly to the bondage of fear in the Limited Self.

4. Worry annihilates the experience of the NOW for a future that will never be.

5. Worry creates endocrinal changes that can lead to disease.

So why do we worry? Like many pernicious habits, worry often originates in the early environment. One or both parents, or other intimates, may have used this emotional strategy as a coping mechanism. While the imprints of early childhood often leave their mark, for better or for worse, we can be free of the shackles that bind or hinder us. *Anything* that has originated in early childhood or at another time in life can be transformed with patient, daily practice.

Introspection – Determine Fact from Fiction

The first step in your journey toward becoming free of worry is the cultivation of greater awareness. How are you using your thoughts throughout the day? Are you primarily conscious and choosing the positive, or are you primarily unconscious about your state of mind?

To examine your circumstances clearly, and to break the worry habit, you need to determine what is factual and what is imagined. Consider whether your negative thoughts center on worry over a loved one, or other conditions and circumstances. Are they real conditions or based on assumptions? Are you a central player in some imagined, envisioned, dismal future? Are you projecting powerful negative sequences on a mental screen that has the power of energy in projected reality? That energy is creating in the Now, so it is important to know how you perceive our ability to access peace, joy, or happiness in the present moment.

Re-patterning the Worry Habit

Remember that the mind is pliable. If you are not happy with your mental habits, you can change them by following a step-by-step process:

1. First, analyze your thought patterns. Pay particular attention to worry, anxiety, and negative projection onto present and future.

2. Next, analyze what you worry about. Write down the themes and anxieties that occur in that circular cycle of worry.

3. Now write down your major fears and anxieties. Categorize them according to the general subject matter, such as relationships, finances, love, health, or misfortune. Include also thoughts around lost opportunities and future negative projections.

4. Analyze the worries that receive the most attention due to their frequency and regularity. Take the general thoughts and see what themes are most regularly repeated.

5. Finally, employ spiritualized affirmations to transform the worry habit. Utilize affirmations that state positive, expansive reality other than the negative thought processes in your worry cycle. Write down the affirmation(s) and practice deep, regular repetition, focusing, when possible, on the spiritual centers (spiritual eye in the center of the forehead and slightly above the eyebrows, or medulla oblongata at the base of the skull).

The mind is receptive to change. By substituting positive thoughts for your negative thoughts and ideas, you effectively make permanent changes in your thinking. You no longer self-sabotage. Instead you learn how to channel this energy into creative possibilities. Remember also that affirmations are not merely an expression of shallow positive thinking. They result in great power, spiritual alignment, integration, and a deep attunement with Spirit.

When you begin your journaling session, these or similar questions may be helpful:

- Are there negative subjects or themes you worry about related to your life partner? Your family? Your children?
- Are there specific fears that you project into worry about the significant relationships in your life?
- Are there worry patterns around your work, your career, or financial circumstances?
- Do you focus on worries about your health? Do you ever visualize yourself as sick in the future?

After you have completed your negative list, then create a list of positive affirmations which affirm spiritual truth. Remember, affirmations work not because of faith or belief but because the powerful vibration carried in the word allows you to access the energy of the universe and Spirit. That creative flow and power helps to unlock your own self-knowing. Spiritual initiates have understood the power of affirmations for eons; religious doctrines are based on this concept. Prayer beads and rosaries are simple counting systems for such repetitive statements. Initiates sit for hours, days, and years chanting mantras and programming their minds with spiritual truths.

Truth echoed in sound also creates greater alignment between the Limited Self and the Eternal Self. For a deeper discussion and proper practice of affirmations see my *The Affirmation Handbook: An Energy Charged Path to Growth*, or my *Creating Deliberate Happiness: The Complete Guide*, or consult Paramahansa Yogananda's seminal work on the subject, *Scientific Healing Affirmations*.

Here is the ritual for your Break the Worry Habit practice, to be performed every day for three weeks:

- **Journaling for 15 minutes on Breaking the Worry Habit.**
- **Positive introspection on the theme.**
- **Affirmations for the Second Step**:

*I am confident. I generate and exude the power of confidence
I am confident Now.*

Or

*I am a master
of my conditions
and circumstances
because I am supported
by the universe and the Divine*

Pair your affirmation with a thought for the day such as this one from the visionary physician and healer Deepak Chopra: "*Holding on to anything is like holding on to your breath. You will suffocate. The only way to get anything in the physical universe is by letting go of it. Let go and it will be yours forever.*"

Stepping Stone #3
Learn to be Present in the now

Learning to focus on the present moment to re-center, realign, and claim the power of your creative self.

When we worry, we project circumstances into the future that have not yet occurred. We are living completely outside the present moment in some imagined events that may never come to pass! When our consciousness is absorbed in the present moment, occupied fully on what we are doing now, it cannot also be in future negative circumstances. It is impossible to be engaged in the present and at the same time entertain negative future projections.

Introspection Opportunity

Analyze thought patterns as they pertain to living life now.

- Are your thoughts focusing upon your life now, or do you spend considerable time mentally revisiting the past?
- How much time is spent in projections onto an unseen future?
- Do you frequently reflect on your interior states of inner peace?
- Do you possess feelings of invigorated attunement with life and Spirit?

If you find you are living too much in the past or in the future, you are inadvertently robbing yourself of the riches of peace and well-being that belong only in the present moment. The amount of time spent in anxiety, worry or mental projections has a powerful impact on your life. Scan yourself to see whether your negative refrains are disproportionate to the positive ones in your visualizations. Statements you make to yourself about your unworthiness, lack of deservedness, failures, body-image, etc. can take the limelight away from the good you have accomplished. These "weed thoughts" choke the garden of possibility! You need to examine and uproot them.

Your ability to consistently materialize the fruits of your thoughts, visualizations, and affirmations depends on your continued inner work and knowing that this is an on-going process. Quick-fix remedies may momentarily feel good, or may even yield small incremental results, but they do not uproot long-standing thought patterns with you for years, or a lifetime. The time and effort spent cultivating your own consciousness is the true road to personal empowerment and happiness, to the glorious release of living in the NOW!

Releasing the Past

How many times have you heard, "The past is gone," yet continue to relive some portion of it year after year? One thing is certain: Replaying the past will never alter one day of the now. All of the energy spent in mentally replaying harmful events from the past weakens the energy available to you in the present, creating stagnation in your spiritual evolution and journey. Replaying the past dissipates your strength to create a more powerful NOW. As the spiritually evolved novelist, Leo Tolstoy, so aptly put it: *"Remember then: there is only one time that is important—Now! It is the most important time because it is the only time when we have any power."* Benefits can result from revisiting the past for the purpose of personal inventory, psychological awareness and the sincere desire to change. Reflection and introspection about the past can help, but when this is done to excess, you stay locked in the past. It is only a change of attitude towards past events that can reconcile them and bring the inner peace we seek.

One thing is certain: the future will unfold in a different manner than we anticipate. Our only moment is now. All possibilities originate in the now.

Developing Self-Love

Your nature longs for love, for to be human is to want to share and exchange intimacy. Yet do you really live life being fully present with yourself and others? Is there a strange disconnect within that manifests as a lack of intimacy and connectedness in the now?

You can improve our moment-to-moment engagement with life and others first by increasing your intimacy with yourself. This develops over time as you become more conscious of your thoughts, feelings and internal motivations—each moment. This intimacy with yourself brings self-knowledge. With continued repetition and deepening attention, you can gradually develop this ability as a dependable life-skill. Ultimately, this leads to self-mastery. When you are comfortable in your own skin—regardless of your successes or failings—you can rest in the moment more easily. You are not inclined to seek distractions to cover up your distress. And then, you can love others more fully and intimately.

Mindfulness in the Moment

Keeping your consciousness focused on your moment-to-moment actions and activities takes patient practice. We all live in a society offering every imaginable diversion. Your energy, like every one else's, can easily become scattered, dissipated. Instead, vow to be mindful throughout the day. Mindfulness focuses the attention on the here and now.

To help you develop the practice of living in the moment, you can practice a form of mindfulness meditation. With mindfulness meditation, you take on the role of an impartial observer of everything that passes before your attention. Your intention is not to be focused, but rather to be mindful—that is, to be fully aware and awake to what is going on in the present moment. The breath may anchor you to the present moment, but apart from that, no attempt is made to direct the attention.

Whatever thoughts, so called distractions, sounds, images, ideas, or feelings arise, nothing is excluded. Everything is welcomed. You simply pay attention to whatever is there. You do not judge or evaluate; you simply observe. Whatever happens is okay—you just sit quietly and continue observing.

Mindfulness meditation can be applied to all experiences in life. Whatever is happening, you should not try to separate yourself from the experience outside yourself. Mindfulness is about embracing reality and the present moment, whether we are working, running or enjoying a meal.

When you become more aware of your present thoughts and feelings, you begin to learn how you are defining yourself, often without realizing it. Awareness is a powerful revealer of the hidden. If you replay and repeat negative past events that dissipate your life energy, your will power, enthusiasm and inspiration, you will begin to see that habit of thought more clearly. Only then can you start the process of releasing those thoughts and allowing a new reality to take shape within.

You need to claim your full potential NOW. Remember, for maximum positive results, you must affirm the spiritual truth from a place of powerful co-creation with life, the universe, and the Divine, (for example, "I co-create powerfully with the Divine."

Re-programming the human brain takes practice and persistence. You did not create mental habits overnight. Likewise, neither you nor anyone else can change long-standing habits quickly. But the good news is that the more you practice, the more you remember to practice and the easier it becomes. You begin to notice when worry or negative self-talk arises. As soon as you begin to catch your thoughts and understand the underlying core belief, the more readily you can release both the thought and the belief, and then establish new beliefs through the use of spiritualized affirmations.

Again you will accelerate your foundational change if for three weeks, you practice Being in the Now by moving through these practical exercises every day.

- **Journaling for 15 minutes on Being in the Now.**
- **Positive introspection.**
- **Affirmations for the Third Step:**

I am radiant, endless,
vibrant, electric energy and youth
in every cell and atom
of my being NOW
(by John Laurence)

Or

I am fully present
with my divine self
in my physical form. NOW.

Pair your affirmation with a thought such as: "Worries are phantoms. The past is history, the future is mystery. Live in the NOW."

Stepping Stone #4
Develop the Art of Forgiveness

A powerful, effective way to truly claim your expansive power and to relinquish the memories and emotions associated with old injuries

Being a human being often means experiencing painful situations and difficult people. You may have suffered an injustice—physical or emotional injury—any of the countless circumstances that challenge us.

You should not discount or minimize your painful or even destructive experiences. What happened to you does matter. You have the right to feel injured. You have the right to grieve and to mourn your loss of potential or opportunity. More importantly, however, you also have the power, the ability, and the capacity to free yourself from these old injuries, however severe or debilitating. You do this with forgiveness and by releasing the past. The act of forgiving allows you to begin to discover who you are, released from the intense binding chains that hold us to a remote time.

Forgiveness is also a conscious decision to remove the power from individuals or circumstances of the past. By the act of forgiveness you transfer your power back to yourself. By forgiving past injuries you begin to empower yourself for the act of forgiveness which:

- will unlock your innate power.
- will allow you to redefine yourself.
- will lessen the power over your life by any who injured you.
- will move your energy and life force in a positive direction.

Introspection/Journaling Opportunity

In your journal, examine any experience in which you felt you were damaged, or victimized, by another. Write down why you are angry with that person and at events or circumstances. Write down why you are angry with yourself and what you do to begin to forgive yourself.

As you shift your perceptions of anger directed at others, your self and/or circumstances, you create the possibility of a new paradigm that may allow you to:

1. Redefine yourself with a more positive self-image.
2. Redefine circumstances.
3. Give you permission to be happier and to experiment with joy.
4. Release energy that will allow you to extend greater forgiveness to yourself.
5. Unlock the creative force within you for acts of new creation.

Why Do We Resist Forgiving?

You may have difficulty forgiving because, at some level, you may feel that you are minimizing or disregarding injuries from the past. All events that involve significant injury to another individual, or other individuals, *do matter.* Forgiveness does not negate the importance of the injury; what occurred is indelible in the reality in which it occurred. But you reclaim your great power simply by reframing the past with a shift in your consciousness and perspective. You create an exit strategy for strongly imprisoned feelings and emotions of blocked possibilities.

Sometimes anger can masquerade as a sense of power. You may be afraid that relinquishing your anger is a sign of weakness: "If I forgive, will I be giving up? Will I lose a part of myself to the perpetrator?" This is a mistaken perception. Forgiveness does not limit your power. It vastly increases it! Forgiveness is an aspect of love. Nothing is more powerful than the vibration of love. You may not be able to arrive at that place where you love your enemy. But staying in a place of hatred or dislike diminishes your power. Unknowingly, you give the perpetrator more power, binding your energy to holding onto the act or circumstances that injured you in the first place. By that focus and preoccupation, you build a continuous bridge of connection to the past, and as a consequence, your own energy field is less free to participate in its own possibilities now and in the future. You should never allow someone else to have that power over you. You always have the power to release yourself from the past by making the decision to forgive.

Forgiveness may also be difficult because of a mistaken notion that forgiveness releases the individual from accountability. Your act of forgiveness does not change the accountability of others. What took place is forever written in the Eternal. All of us are accountable for our thoughts, actions, and deeds. True accountability is beyond the rules of man. Spiritual law states that energy expended in a positive or negative manner must, in some way, be returned to the source of origin. The timing of the universe and the events involved in that law of accountability is absolute. Only the interceding law of grace may alter the inevitable outcomes in the lives of individuals. In life, "a person reaps what he sows." (Gal. 6:7)

Note: Sometimes we may find ourselves dealing with such a deep level of emotion that it is difficult to find our way to forgiveness on our own. In certain circumstances, it may be helpful to seek the help of a licensed therapist or counselor to provide perspective and help ease us into a place from which we can release the past.

Self-Forgiveness

Forgiving ourselves for the "mistakes" of being human.

Usually we make the best decisions and the best choices that we are able to make according to our understanding and evolution at any given time. As we grow, our understanding and discernment deepens. Of course, if that same understanding were present in the past, we might have made entirely different choices and experienced a different outcome. Nevertheless, we did our best at the time. Hopefully, the insight we gain from the past has given us a greater awareness of consequences from our earlier choices. If the blind man acquires new sight, should he be judged for the trips and falls he made when he could not see?

Part of forgiving yourself involves accepting this truth: that you acted upon your own best knowledge at the time. If you have progressed to a greater place of insight and understanding, what purpose does it serve to blame yourself? You have acquired new sight. You now have the power to move that knowledge forward toward personal change. You have the capacity to learn from your mistakes. Such lessons become solid ground beneath your feet, supporting you on the path of life. Those lessons also help you develop compassion for the human struggles we all share with one another.

Sometimes you may experience unresolved anger at "self" for not being able to deflect the damage that occurred. Sometimes you may expect yourself to have the power of God and the power of the universe. You may develop shame and guilt because you were "guilty" of being human, of being a child, or of being vulnerable to someone else.

Part of your power is the power to forgive yourself for not being all-knowing, all-powerful, at all moments in time. Behind all anger are other emotions which tie to hurt, sadness, disappointment. In the *Bhagavad Gita*, a central element of Yogic and Vedic philosophy, anger is considered the natural outcome of thwarted desire, of things not going the way we would like. There may be times when you are in touch with your anger but not in touch with the underlying core feelings of anger at yourself. Feelings of embarrassment, shame, sadness, and disappointment may accompany that anger because you felt powerless to anticipate, or prevent, the injury that occurred.

When it's difficult to forgive yourself, try to recognize that prolonged anger against the self, any form of self-loathing only intensifies those feelings and creates a vicious cycle. The less these feeling states are recognized, the more they have the power to fester and grow. Self-contempt develops. And from self-contempt there may be a progression to self-loathing. Self-loathing further diminishes self-esteem. Self-esteem issues may also further complicate your commitment to forgive yourself.

Forgiveness Practice: Healing Relationship Wounds

- Mentally visualize the individual with whom you desire to achieve more healing. Encircle them in your mind with white light.
- Begin with an invocation of your preference, i.e., "Dear God," "Divine Source," "Universal Power," "Heal and bless _____ (name of individual)."
- Repeat that several times.
- Then say "May the divine power of the universe now bless, heal and elevate the conditions and circumstances in the life of _____ (name of individual)."
- After you have envisioned the encircling of the individual in the light, repeat this technique with yourself at the center of that light.
- Repeat that several times: "Divine source, bless and heal me."
- Follow this with: "May the divine power of the universe bless, heal and elevate the conditions and circumstances of my life now." For greatest results, repeat this exercise several times a day with will-charged energy and intention.

Please note: Petitions or requests for improved circumstances, whether in relationships, conditions, health, healing, or greater spiritual attunement, should always be stated in the "Now". Know that the Divine Source of all things desires that we be full participants in life and is always working with us toward the elevation of our consciousness.

Again you will accelerate your foundational change and move toward forgiveness if, for three weeks, you practice Forgiveness by moving through these practical exercises every day.

- **Journaling for 15 minutes on cultivating Forgiveness.**
- **Positive introspection on this theme.**
- **Affirmations for the Fourth Step:**

I forgive all injuries as I would be forgiven.
I am a friend to all.
Empathy and understanding
are my essence.
Love is my nature.

Or

I am becoming
the heart itself,
merging in love
with humanity,
with myself,
with God.

Pair it with a thought on forgiveness such as the wonderful Mark Twain quote: "Forgiveness is the fragrance the violet sheds on the heel that has crushed it."

Stepping Stone #5
Reframing Experiences

Your experiences are a combination of actual events and your interpretation of those events, in other words, the emphasis and perception you place on them. No event is without interpretation. The nature of the mind is to sort through and learn from experiences. In your journaling you have been writing about your thoughts, feelings, lessons, longings, progress and setbacks. To take your journaling deeper, let's look at how you personally relate to what happens in your life — in other words, look at your *relationship* to the experiences you have.

Two people can go through the identical experiences but have vastly different reactions. How do you personally experience loss? Does it take weeks or months to recover your equilibrium? Can you find inner resilience more quickly? Are you philosophical about change and difficulty? Or do you take things very seriously, look at "the glass half empty" or hold on to old hurts through the years?

Regardless of how you answer these questions, reframing your experiences will help you to move forward in life with greater perspective, inner peace and personal growth. No time machine will take you back to the past and shift the events themselves. Your power lies in reframing. In this way, events or major themes in your life are considered from a new, healthier and more empowered perspective. As you reframe, you recreate the energy around the experience and your relationship to it.

This does not mean that areas of disappointment, adversity, or tragedy in life do not matter, or that the experiences of sorrow, sadness, loss and heartbreak are without significance.

As an aid to begin reframing, focus on the event or experience and ask yourself this question: "Is there anything positive, or of benefit, that can be derived from it?" For example:

- Has your understanding been increased?

- Has your capacity for sympathy or empathy for others been positively altered or expanded?
- Is there any area in which you have reached out more to others after undergoing some difficulty?
- Did you learn more about yourself?
- Did you learn more about others?
- What are your intentions regarding that information? As you make a new intention, you begin to create a new experience.
- Do you have a greater ability and power to be a contributor in the here and now? The first step is to contribute to yourself!

Sometimes the art of reframing experiences may be as simple as identifying one or more benefits from an otherwise negative or painful experience. Then you continue to place great energy and focus on those benefits in order to recreate the experience in a more positive light. Instead of the circular pattern of replaying the negative, you can begin establishing a circular pattern of replaying the newly created positive. Your most severe pain may be the beginning of a new healing perspective. It may give you the gift of appreciation.

Reframing is dependent on your faith in the possibility of change. Not all situations and circumstances can be changed of course. However, you have immense power to change your thoughts about your circumstances. I have always found inspiration in these words of Vicktor Frankl, who, despite his three years in a concentration camp (1942-45), found an indomitable strength in the power of free choice: *"The last of human freedoms,"* he wrote, *"is the ability to choose one's attitude in a given set of circumstances."* While his were extreme circumstances, his example is a testament to the power of choice. By cultivating forgiveness, wisdom, detachment, renewed hope and gratitude you, too, can powerfully transform even the most difficult experiences.

Again you will accelerate your ability to positively reframe your experiences if, for three weeks, you practice this reframing as you move through these practical exercises every day.

- **Journaling for 15 minutes on Reframing Experiences.**
- **Positive introspection on this theme of positive choice.**
- **Affirmations for the Fifth Step:**

My rightful intention
aligns Myself with Truth.
My rightful intention
changes the universe.
My rightful intention
changes myself.

Or

I am a master
of my conditions
and circumstances
because I am supported
by the universe and the Divine.

Pair your affirmation with a thought for the day such as this quotation from Paramahansa Yogananda about thought assuming tangible form:

"Consciousness is imaginative, sensitive and pliable; it can think and dream itself into any state."

Stepping Stone #6
Cultivate the Habit of Gratitude

Developing the habit of gratitude lays a foundation for the development of devotion, which is the portal to the Divine.

Gratitude is a training ground for the consciousness. When we live in an attitude of gratitude, we are predisposed to see the good, however small, in each moment. Without fail, surveying, analyzing, and assessing circumstances in the Now, with gratitude, will bring about an increase in your happiness. *"Gratitude brings delight,"* wrote Sharon Salzman in her book *Loving Kindness*. Circumstances may or may not be changing, but gratitude helps you retain what is positive from an experience.

Gratitude also breaks circular patterns of mental negativity. It is directly at odds and wholly incompatible with the emotions of powerlessness and victimhood. The habit of gratitude uproots tenacious, unhealthy and restrictive thought patterns.

Developing an awareness of your blessings is life transforming. "I am grateful for these eyes that see, these ears that hear, these hands that touch, these legs that walk, etc." You can also say, "I am grateful for this moment in time while I am experiencing it NOW." Using expressions of gratitude and appreciation will increase the happiness in your life, regardless of circumstances. Evidence for this comes from a fascinating project on gratitude and thankfulness called *Dimensions and Perspectives of Gratitude*. Conducted at the University of California at Davis, the project focused on two main lines of inquiry: (1) developing methods to cultivate gratitude in daily life and to assess gratitude's effect on well-being, and (2) developing a measure to reliably assess individual differences in dispositional gratefulness. Researchers found that those who practiced gratitude and kept a weekly journal, exercised more regularly, reported fewer physical symptoms, felt better about their lives as a whole, and were more optimistic about the upcoming week compared to those who recorded hassles or neutral life events (Emmons & McCullough, 2003).

"People with a strong disposition toward gratitude have the capacity to be empathic and to take the perspective of others," the study concluded. "They are rated as more generous and more helpful by people in their social networks (McCullough, Emmons, & Tsang, 2002)."

Too often you may feel you will be happy only when the big changes occur in your life. The truth is, when you learn to attend to small blessings in the Now, your gratitude expands these blessings into important gifts. Gratitude begets gratitude. You consciousness will move from gratitude and appreciation to a greater connection with Spirit, with yourself, with life, with others.

Gratitude makes us move from the Limited Self, which sees itself as the primary "doer," into the realm of the expansive Eternal Self. Your connection with Spirit is cultivated by the act of gratitude. Because gratitude involves some recognition of a Source beyond oneself, it creates the groundwork for devotion. The act of devotion is simply acknowledging your connection with the Divine. Devotion heightens your capacity to interact with and express through the Eternal Self.

In Gratitude: A Poem

*In gratitude
I claim the Now.
Expansively I draw
New life into me
And see the Radiant Light of All.*

*In gratitude I see
The unseen hand
Guiding me, guiding you.
In gratitude
I take the hand
It lifts us ever higher
To the vision of ourselves.
In gratitude I give,
Expansively I exude the Now.*

Again you will accelerate your ability to cultivate gratitude if, for three weeks, you cultivate those seeds as you move through these practical exercises every day. During this sixth week, I ask you to add a brief meditation to your practice of each step. For now, simply sit quietly with both feet on the floor, spine straight, eyes closed, focusing the internal eye on the object of your gratitude — one sense, person, experience or gift for which you feel grateful. Stepping Stone #7 will offer more meditation techniques. But for these three weeks, simply sit quietly for a time each day focused on feeling gratitude.

- **Meditating for at least 10 minutes on gratitude.**
- **Journaling for 15 minutes on this same theme.**
- **Introspection on all the reasons you have to be grateful.**

- **Affirmations for Sixth Step:**

I give thanks
for daily my power
of dynamic will strengthens.
I am led to the light
and to the right
by divine attunement.
Give me the attunement to receive,
and perceive,
and to act in Your holy name.

Or

I give thanks for
I am a magnet of success.
God is opening doors
of opportunity NOW.

Pair your affirmation with a quotation such as "Be thankful for the difficult times. During those times you grow."

Stepping Stone #7
Penetrate into the Stillness

> *If the doors of perception were cleansed, everything would appear to us as it is, Infinite.*
>
> William Blake

All beings, no matter how reactionary, fearful, violent or lost, can open themselves to the sacred within and become free. Spirit is our very being. Meditation allows us access to the deeper regions of our spiritual nature, connects us with the Divine presence within, and provides us a clearer vision of the truth. Scheduling time each day for meditation practice is essential not only for peace and well-being, but for experiencing our Eternal Selves, the true source of lasting happiness. There are countless meditation techniques available and myriad philosophies about the proper method of meditation. Finding an effective and suitable style of meditation for you can take time and experimentation but will prove invaluable. I offered one technique in Chapter One, but repeat elements of that technique here.

Meditation Technique

The proper posture for meditation is very important.

- Sitting in a straight back chair is recommended.

- The feet should be flat on the floor, pointed straight ahead.

- In a state of relaxation, maintain a straight spine, to the best of your ability without straining or discomfort.

- Place your hands, with palms turned gently upward, near the junction between your legs and thighs. (Note: Meditation techniques, in general, should not be practiced in a position where the individual is lying down in a bed. When lying down, the meditative state too easily becomes a sleep state.

If an individual has the physical ability to sit either in a chair with feet flat on the floor—or cross-legged on the floor on a flat surface, the sitting posture should be assumed. In general avoid sitting on a bed, for consciousness usually associates the bed with sleep.)

This meditation technique involves focusing your attention at the point between the eyebrows known as the "spiritual eye." This is a center that increases our spiritual connectedness as we focus upon it. If you are having difficulty in achieving or maintaining the proper eye position for your meditation, the following suggestion may assist you in getting the correct angle for your focus gaze. The eyes should be turned gently and slightly upward.

Pencil Technique for Proper Gaze

Visualize holding a #2 pencil eraser at the spiritual eye. Visualize the eraser resting on the forehead between and slightly above the eyebrows, centered at the spiritual eye, with the pencil parallel to the ground. Allow your focus to move to where you visualize the point of the pencil to be. Keep the gaze focused at that spot. This technique is not part of the practice itself, but will prevent you from placing excessive strain on the eyes and help develop a better habit pattern for meditation.

Preparation for Meditation

- Visualize that you are encircled by white light that either outlines the body or is shaped as a spherical egg-shape. Have the <u>intention</u> of placing white light around the body, for the intention is what summons a greater connection with Spirit and strengthens the energy field.
- After visualizing the white light in this way, begin to observe the breath in a relaxed state of mind. Maintain the correct posture with spine erect and feet flat on the floor.

- Affirm that you are divinely protected by the surrounding white light of Spirit. (Example: "I am surrounded by the light field of the Divine. I am ever protected. I am ever embraced by the Divine Force.") Repeat this protection affirmation, or a similar one, five or six times.

- Now, in this relaxed state of mind, begin to observe the breath without any attempt to regulate it. Neither speed up nor slow down the rhythm of the breath. Simply observe the inhalation and exhalation as it naturally flows in and out.

- See yourself as "piggy-backing" on each inhalation and exhalation. Mentally say, "I ride the inward breath." As you naturally begin to exhale, mentally say "I ride the outward breath." Continue this pattern for approximately 15 minutes. Visualize yourself riding the inward breath and the outward breath. Then change the repetition of words on the inhaling and exhaling breath to "I am That".

Additional affirmations that may be mentally repeated prior to or following the use of this meditation technique:

> *I ride the inward breath.*
> *I ride the outward breath.*
> *I am one with that breath.*
> *Reveal Thyself,*

Note: Effective meditation techniques are available from Self-Realization Fellowship in the form of lessons that are delivered to your home every two weeks.

For information contact:

Self-Realization Fellowship
3880 San Rafael Drive
Los Angeles, CA 90065-3219
323-225-2471
http//www.yogananda-srf.org

Again you will accelerate your ability to penetrate stillness if, for three weeks, you practice meditation, journaling and these other components of your ritual of transformation every day.

- **Meditating for a minimum of 10 minutes.**
- **Journaling for 15 minutes on this theme.**
- **Positive introspection.**
- **Repeating Affirmations for Seventh Step**:

You may choose an affirmation guiding breath or focus or create an affirmation of your own. Here are two possibilities:

I mount
the incoming breath.
I ride to the end.
I let the breath
begin its descent
while I mount for the
downward ride.
I ride the breath
of mind.

Or

Still lake of peace,
I drink tranquility.
I sip waters of knowing.
I penetrate the stillness.

Pair your affirmation with a thought such as this from the Chinese philosopher Lao Tzu: "*To the mind that is still, the whole universe surrenders.*

Stepping Stone #8
Become a Co-Creator with the Divine

You are a being of light entitled to access the limitless streams of light, love, and spiritual power by the creative nature of who you are.

The Stepping Stones to Change create the opportunity for greater alignment and integration of the Limited and the Eternal Self. The more aligned and integrated you are, the more you are able to access your own personal power. Greater alignment unlocks the power of creativity latent within you. Creativity is not an aspect of personality. It is a part of your essence, your divine nature. When you attribute your creative power to an aspect of personality you limit your ability to access your personal power and creativity.

- Ideas about being uncreative, without talent, and insignificant in what you can contribute are tied to identification with the Limited Self and are not grounded in truth. Ideas of a limited creative nature will tend to create limited magnetism and less inspiration and less manifestation.

- When you open to the possibility that the creative force is within, you expand your consciousness. Your creativity is innate and it ties to the origin of your existence. You are not a puppet that God moves. You are not an empty vessel. You are a dynamic, creative being that possesses the creative power of the God-force. You have the ability to harness this creativity, claim it, and manifest it. You not only have the power to be a co-creator with the Divine, you are made for such activity, and as such your potential is unlimited.

- You do not have to have faith or believe that you are a powerhouse of creativity with the ability to harness the creative energy of the universe. You need only affirm that it is so and act on this truth to the best of your ability. As you do, you will encourage the eruption of your dynamic force and personal potency co-creating with the inexhaustible Source of creativity.

These Stepping Stones to Change are practical techniques to propel you forward on your path to lasting happiness. Employing these small steps with consistency will lead to giant leaps in transformation. Never despair, for you are not alone on your journey. Spirit is ever with you, supporting and guiding you on the road to happiness. Let no cloud of discouragement halt your journey. Sunlight and the force of all creation is sustaining and uplifting you to the source of your Knowing.

Again you will accelerate your ability to become a co-creator with the divine if, for three weeks, you practice meditation, journaling and these other components of your ritual of transformation every day.

- **Meditating for a minimum of 10 minutes.**
- **Journaling for 15 minutes on themes of creativity.**
- **Positive introspection.**
- **Repeating Affirmations for the Eighth Step**:

The Divine
is the artist within me.
I am the art
of the Artist
ever manifesting.

Or

I am the dynamic force of creativity in the universe. That force and power is expressed through me Now.

Pair your affirmation with a thought for the day centering on the same theme such as "The creative power at once brings the whole universe to order."

Affirmations to Enhance the Stepping Stones to Change

For Manifesting My Spiritual Light
My spiritual light,
in divine brilliance,
is manifesting.
My capacity to see
and perceive
that light
in others
is ever expanding.

For Moderation in All Things
O' compassionate One,
walk with me
on the pathway
of the middle ground.
Reason and moderation
are guideposts
for me Now.

For Awakening to the Voice of God
The breath of God enfolds me, caresses me, awakens me.

For Riding the Breath Like a Wave
I ride the inward breath.
I ride the outward breath.
I am one with that breath.
Reveal Thyself, O' Divine Essence.
(Relax. Practice seeing yourself as riding on the breath. Do not control the breathing.)

For Surfing the Breath's Flow
I ride the breath
in my mind's eye.
I follow the breath
like a resident rider
of moving flow.

For Riding the Rhythm of Breath and Mind
I mount
the incoming breath.
I ride to the end.
I let the breath
begin its descent
while I mount for the
downward ride.
I ride the breath
of mind.

For Protection in the Light
I am surrounded
by the light field of the Divine.
I am ever protected.
I am ever embraced
by the Divine Force

For Riding to Joy and Knowing
I ride the breath waves
to perfect joy
and bliss knowing.
I am peace.
I am joy.
I am bliss.

Thoughts for the Day: A Sampler

Your life can be enriched and empowered by adding a positive, powerful thought to your daily practice of affirmations. The following thoughts are taken from a variety of sources worldwide. Some may appeal to you. And, of course, you may discover your own thought for the day in your own reading or experience.

> *As the mind and the feelings are directed inward, you begin to feel God's joy. The pleasures of the senses do not last; but the joy of God is everlasting. It is incomparable!*
>
> PARAMAHANSA YOGANANDA

> *A bird does not sing because it has an answer. It sings because it has a song.*
>
> CHINESE PROVERB

> *Let your hopes, not your hurts, shape your future.*
>
> ROBERT H. SCHULLER

> *Attachment is blinding; it lends an imaginary halo of attractiveness to the object of desire.*
>
> SRI SWAMI YUKTESWAR

> *This is my simple religion. There is no need for temples; no need for complicated philosophy. Our own brain, our own heart is our temple; the philosophy is kindness.*
>
> HIS HOLINESS, THE DALAI LAMA

To the mind that is still, the whole universe surrenders.
LAO TZU

We can make our minds so like still water that beings gather about us that they may see, it may be, their own images and so live for a moment with a clearer, perhaps even with a fiercer life because of our quiet.
W. B. YEATS

The laughter of the infinite God must vibrate through your smile. Let the breeze of His love spread your smiles in the hearts of men. Their fire will be contagious.
PARAMAHANSA YOGANANDA

The fullness of joy is to behold God in everything.
JULIAN OF NORWICH

The ocean refuses no river.
VEDIC WISDOM

As rivers flow into the sea, losing their individuality, so the enlightened, no longer bound by name and form, merge with the infinite, the radiant Cosmic Being.
BRIHADARANYAKA UPANISHAD

Blonde-Haired Girl Holding Yellow Flowers
By Yvonne G. Christenson

CHAPTER 3

MANIFESTATION: FROM THE INSIDE OUT

THE LAW OF MAGNETISM AND MANIFESTATION

Many who sincerely desire to change and create a life of greater personal happiness and spiritual awareness nonetheless encounter times of struggle and doubt. Feelings of disappointment and unworthiness arise when sincere efforts fail to yield timely results. You may await the promised power of manifestation and materialization with great anticipation. Yet others appear to be achieving, almost effortlessly, while you engage in laborious, fruitless work. This can create a cycle of self-blame and negative self-talk.

The powerful force of your own self-concept regarding your worthiness, right to receive, and deservedness underlies your present circumstances. Simply said, you are what you think. With your thoughts, you make your world. The beauty of this is that you can alter these conceptions and reclaim your divine nature as a child of God. Yet true change takes time and you must persevere in your pursuit if you are to manifest your cherished dreams and goals. Unrealistic expectations and promises about the "magic" of change can only lead to disappointment.

It is heartening to understand this truth: *We have the power to change! We have a vast reservoir of power within us that is tied directly to the Source of all creation. This is the true magic of manifestation.*

To repeat: We have a vast reservoir of power within. When combined with consistency of effort, application of techniques, persistence in practice, and continuing personal assessment and re-evaluation, your success is assured. You will attain the results of the spiritual laws associated with the physical plane as well as an ever-greater awakening of your soul's nature. Perseverance is key. It is your commitment to stay the course that will bring the greatest reward.

If, on the other hand, you believe that, by mere intention and visualization techniques alone, we can effortlessly produce and manifest what we desire, you may be sorely disappointed and discouraged.

Six Steps in the Process of Powerful Manifestation

1. **Inspiration and imagination:** Spiritual power is activated by the combination of these two elements. They coalesce to form an idea. This begins the stirring into motion of spiritual force.

2. **Idea:** An idea is a not yet fully energized thought form. Ideas derive from inspiration and the gift of imagination. They are crystallized inspiration taking form; energized movement from a sea of Spirit.

3. **Dynamic intention:** Dynamic intention can become energized and move as a volitional force by the activity of dynamic will.

4. **Dynamic visualization:** A thought image, sketched in the light, becomes energized with Spirit or energized imagination.

5. **Dynamic affirmations:** Spiritualized power encased in words and directed by concentrated, focused will power. Words infused with the spirit of creation move toward manifestation.

6. **Manifestation:** The materialized aspect of an idea. Points 3, 4, 5 are all Spirit-based and bring vital creative energy to the process of manifestation. Dynamic will power infuses an idea with an irresistible charged energy.

From Idea to Manifestation

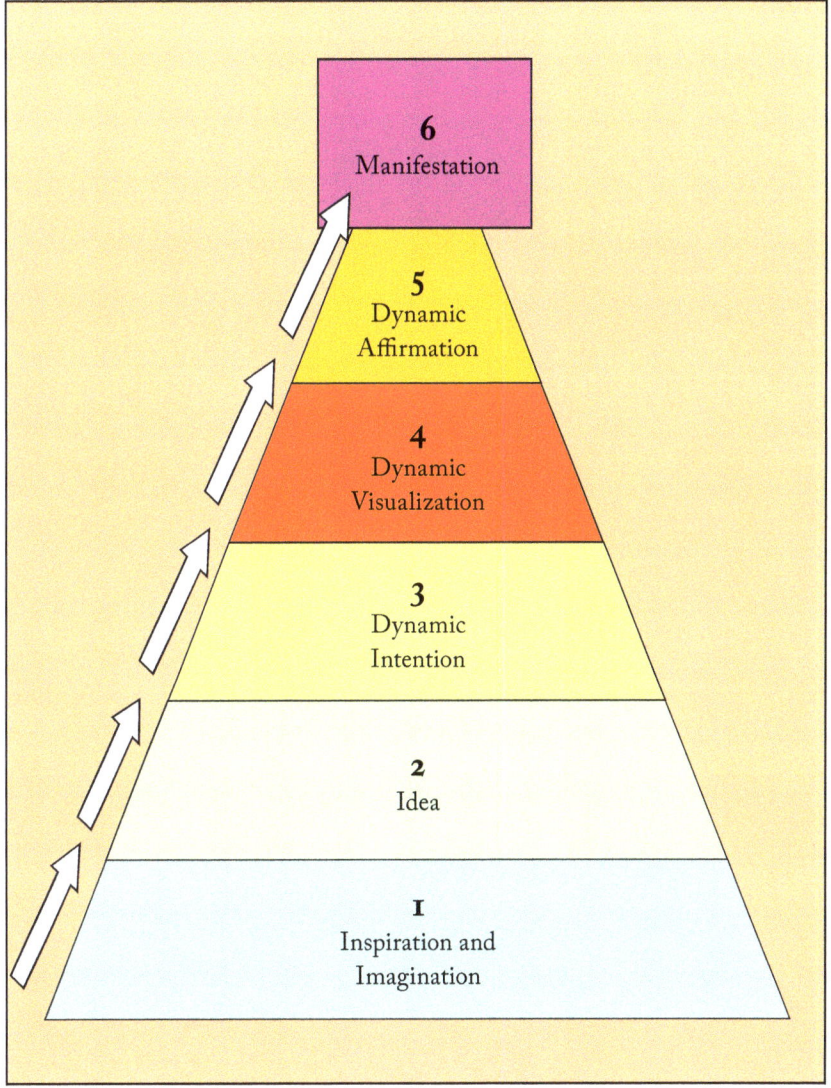

There are subtle yet profound spiritual laws at play in the process of manifestation. To manifest your dreams and goals is a process akin to the very laws of creation itself. Creation operates via the Laws of Magnetism and the Laws of Attraction.

Your attitudes impact your prosperity

There is a direct relationship between your attitudes and that which is attracted to you through the law of magnetism and attraction.

Attitudes to cultivate include:

1. The attitude of gratitude and appreciation.
2. The attitude of thankfulness.
3. A positive attitude towards the prosperity of others.

Your attitudes are the road upon which prosperity and abundance travel. Your attitudes project dynamic energy, and have the power to attract circumstances by the law of magnetism. Your present circumstances can be altered and changed by paying close attention to the habit patterns that exist within you in your thoughts.

Introspection

- Write down your attitudes and ideas around how you see prosperity and abundance in your life. Gaining clarity about how your individualized thought patterns cluster into broad attitudes will give you specific target areas to address.

- Write down what you say to yourself when good fortune and prosperity suddenly occur.

- Write down what you say to yourself when unexpected financial reverses, or states of lack, dominate your life. This will help you gain insight into your attitudes and thoughts.

The attitude of gratitude and appreciation

You are part of a bigger picture. When you begin to see yourself as a part of the stream of good by which the divine flow moves, you will access not only your own supply but also an ability and willingness to supply others. When you see all that you have as coming from your own efforts, or your ability to make others supply your wants, needs, and desires, then you may tighten your grip into a greater fear of lack. Your efforts have been important and your participation has been vital to that which has manifested in your life; it did not originate in a vacuum. But heightening your awareness that you are part of a larger flow of limitless abundance will increase your capacity to experience increased flow in consciousness and circumstances with others.

Whatever your present level of flow, still practice the habits of gratitude and appreciation as outlined in Stepping Stone #6. To feel more gratitude, bring to your mind from past memories a situation or circumstance in which you felt grateful. Try, by using your imagination, to remember the scene and the feeling state that accompanied that. Keep revolving that theme and that feeling state in your mind. As you are in greater attunement with that feeling, review your present circumstances. To the best of your ability attach that same feeling to situations and experiences in the Now. That technique will increase your ability to feel gratitude in a broader circle of circumstances. Also, even if you do not feel particularly grateful, simply repeat "I am grateful. I am thankful. I am a receiver of the good."

By cultivating attitudes of gratitude and appreciation, the universe will respond. Your positive flow of appreciation will generate, like a magnet, a divine response. Along with cultivating appreciation, also cultivate the habit of saying "thank you" to the Divine Source. Change your relationship to that of being a true co-creator with the divine. See yourself as being abundantly supplied and abundantly supplying.

Visualizing, affirming, and practicing statements of ever-greater faith in possibilities are powerful tools by which the new manifests. Being proactive in changing your consciousness empowers your life.

As your consciousness cultivates, your circumstances manifest. Proceed as if you have the power and the right of access to the limitless good of the earth. Proceed as if God will move in divine response to your intention. Proceed as if you will be successful in penetrating into that vast reservoir of abundant supply. Proceed as if success will be yours, victory and prosperity will be yours. And so shall it be.

Abundance and Prosperity: You Can Make Them Appear

The word "APPEAR" can remind you of areas that need to be examined and focused upon to create new levels of prosperity and abundance.

- **A**nalyze
    a. Analyze your present conditions and circumstances.
    b. Analyze your prosperity consciousness. (Do you believe you have a right to prosper?)
    c. Analyze if you have given yourself *permission* to prosper and access limitless supply. Do you have deep feelings that you do not have a right to succeed and prosper? What is the origin of those thoughts and feelings? Are there deservedness issues with you?

- **P**rioritize
    a. What areas need to be changed?
    b. What positive areas could be further expanded?
    c. Create a change list. Indicate by some system which things require immediate change, and which have less urgency. Everything else will fall into the middle category. This can be listed by doing "1" as the most urgent to change and "3" being the least urgent; everything else is "2." Make a commitment to start with level "1." Then prioritize. Do not go to items labeled as # 2 until you complete the level 1 items.

- **P**erseverance is the repetition of willed activity toward a specific goal or specified direction. Without perseverance there will be minimal creation and action. The act of volition, or movement, is driven by perseverance. Creativity is ignited by the movement of action and ideas, as well as the ability to achieve mastery of goals, ideas, and activities.

- **E**nergize your dynamic intention into purpose-driven activity. Activity needs to be activated by imagination, visualization, and a statement of intention in order for you to be a true co-creator in an abundant exchange with the universe.

- **A**ction is necessary. No change can occur without a decision to take action. Otherwise, dreams remain dreams, and visualized scenes never manifest. Imagination without action limits the possibility of significant change and movement. It remains only in the realm of possibility. From your change list, select any item where you can begin to make changes by taking action. Add to your list what are your fears about what will happen to you if you initiate change in any fashion. The fears about what might occur create non-movement, stagnation, and paralysis of dynamic will.

- **R**esearch. Be willing to investigate and explore information available about areas in which you are interested. If you are considering new endeavors, or new business projects, or new ways of marketing an established product, explore any relevant data. Insufficient information and limited knowledge may limit your ability to go forward. Instead, let your creativity join your exploration of new, relevant information and processes.

Summarizing this process: To create new levels of resources and greater abundance and prosperity, use analysis, permission to prosper, dynamic intention, and dynamic visualization, as well as affirmations, and the habit of gratitude, *as if divine manifestation has already materialized.*

Angels Frolicking Around Large Bells
By Yvonne G. Christenson

CHAPTER 4

CREATIVITY

Creativity is your spiritual birthright. The divinity within you desires to unite with you in the act of co-creation.

Key topics Addressed in this Chapter:

- Creativity is not a specific talent, finite and limited in origin. You possess the spark of creativity within.
- Creativity is part of your spiritual nature, not an attribute of personality.
- Creativity can be accessed by a more harmonious alignment between the Limited Self and the Eternal Self.
- Creativity is harnessed by meditation, visualization, and affirmations, among other techniques.
- Affirmations can dramatically expand your awareness of the creative force and your Eternal Self.

CREATIVITY IS INFINITE

As you learned in Stepping Stone #8, creativity is not an attribute of personality, nor is it limited to a select type of artistic person. Creativity is intrinsically tied to your spiritual nature and ultimately to your happiness. You do not "acquire" it. You simply need to activate that which is already present within. The spark of creativity that ignites the stars, forms universes and gives color to the flowers is within you as well. It makes you feel alive, connected to your human family, to nature, beauty and the cosmos. Creativity provides the deepest sense of joy and well-being. This chapter will expand upon this idea of creativity as your birthright and source of joy, a discussion begun in Stepping Stone #8, and further detailed here.

At times in your life creative effort may seem out of reach. You may cast a longing gaze at the artists of the world thinking you are missing the creative "gene" that was their endowment. Why do some people seem to have greater creative ability than others? If we all do have it, why haven't you been able to abundantly manifest it in your life?

Whether you experience its presence or not, the seed of creativity *is* within. It is part of the cosmic energy of the universe itself, and thus the very origin of your divine nature. You may tap into the expansive flow of creation at any time. Expanding your creative aspect within is a spiritual opportunity and a divine promise.

Like your sense of deservedness, your feelings about your own creativity may have come from messages you received from your family and your culture. Even your own experiences may have led to mistaken ideas about your creative capacity. Changing such ideas will help you create deliberate happiness.

Examples of false ideas about creativity:

- I am not a creative person.
- My creativity is limited.
- I don't have any special creative talents.
- I am not an artist, writer, musician, etc.
- It's too late for me to become creative.
- People are either born creative or they're not.
- I can't be creative and also make money.

- I don't know how to access, or unlock, my creativity.
- I need to be practical and forget creative fulfillment.
- Creativity is impractical and not marketable.
- Creativity is limited and finite, accessible only to a few.
- I cannot express myself creatively, for I am an inferior channel.

Any of these negative ideas can become circular, denying the powerful truth of your innate creativity and your status as a channel of inspiration, beauty, and artistry. You may unlock your creativity and clear that channel by changing your thoughts and self-definition.

What is Creativity?

Creativity is often viewed from too narrow a perspective. You may think of it as simply an attribute of personality, or link it only to specific talents or abilities: "Others are creative; I am not." When you view creativity only as expressed through specific talent areas, you further minimize it by claiming that those talents are impractical.

Creativity can never have narrow constraints or definitions because it is a part of All that Is. It is woven into the very atoms. Every aspect of life springs forth out of the fullness of creativity. As you expand your definition of yourself as a part of all creation, you open to infinite possibilities. You will begin to see yourself as a creative being with unique and potent ways of expressing your personality, talents, insights, and intuition. As you harness your imagination and ride it into the heavenly realm, you no longer will see yourself as a finite expression limited by the body.

In truth, your finite form came from the act of creation. The infinite part of you has never been limited. This understanding frees you to be a co-creator with Life itself. In her book, "The

> *Imagination is the beginning of creation. You imagine what you desire, you will what you imagine and at last you create what you will.*
>
> GEORGE BERNARD SHAW

Zen of Creative Painting," author Jeanne Carbonetti writes, "Creativity is a mystery. That's the great secret to unearthing its treasures. For what you seek to explore and to fathom is really yourself. From the moment you are born, your birthright is to play with the great creative process that is your life."

Creativity Unleashes Your Inherent Power

Creativity is the breath of the gods, giving life, joy, and inspiration to your human existence. It is the bridge between heaven and earth. When you are in tune with your creative nature, you step into another dimension. You explore the heights and depths of your spiritual nature.

The words and attitudes of others, as well as the successes and disappointments of others, have impacted your sense of creativity. If you see yourself as lacking creative talents or the character of an artist, can you identify the origin of such self-assessments? Can you remember specific messages about creative insufficiencies? Was creativity encouraged or discouraged when you were a child?

Regardless of the messages you received as a child, it is never too late to tap into this dynamo within. The brilliant painter, Henry Matisse, succinctly put it this way: "Creativity takes courage." It takes courage to overcome self-doubt, to try new things, to face our vulnerabilities and to embark on new adventures. Creative effort begins with intention. All journeys begin with a focused aim, followed by will-directed activity.

Tools that Enhance Creativity

Several principles and practices, listed below, are the means by which you can open to your creativity, as well as your own self-empowerment. Exploring your consciousness and examining your habitual patterns of thought will help you to access your natural creative abilities.

- **Imagination** – Examine the role imagination and intuition play in your life at present.

- **Self permission** for growth – Open yourself to change and releasing fear.
- **Dynamic intention** – Trust the power within to create what you intend.
- **Dynamic willpower** – Believe that focused intention, fueled by spirit, energizes the power of will.
- **Visualization** – See yourself as a creative being doing creative acts and arriving at creative solutions.
- **Affirmations** – Assert your potency as creator of your destiny.
- **Meditation** – Emphasize your interiorized consciousness.

We all approach our creativity in different ways. For some, walking through nature inspires their inner muse; for others, meditation or listening to music. Your creativity may speak to you in silence or when you visit places of artistic beauty, such as the Louvre. The well known poet, David Whyte, spoke of accessing creativity through a deep inner conversation with yourself: "You've got to find that contact point as an individual. Ask the question, 'Where am I interested? Where, in a very short time, do I become passionate once I've opened up that initial interest? What do I have energy for? And will I have faith enough to actually spend enough time so that I can open up that door into what, to begin with, is a new territory, but eventually becomes my new home?' "

Mahatma Gandhi also reminds us that we have the answers within: **"Everyone who wills can hear the inner Voice. It is within everyone."**

Tuning in to this inner voice and hearing its message will bring forth the deeper clarity you are seeking. Remember that creative expression has no limitation. It is what moves

Creative success, above all, can be defined as that which is joy-producing to your true nature.

you uniquely. What you feel, and how you are moved, will be unlike anyone else's feelings and inspirations. All new inventions began with the spark of unique creativity—bringing something into the world that no one had dreamed of before.

Introspection Exercise

- List five experiences during which you felt, or demonstrated, some form of creativity, even if you were a child at the time. This may include areas of expression such as a poem, a song, a drawing, or perhaps a creative idea or notion.
- List comments that you remember being said about how someone else saw your creative talents.
- Did you hear discouraging or encouraging statements about your creative interests or attempts? Which statements were predominant?
- Did you internalize any of these ideas, thoughts, or experiences? If so, which ones?
- Did any inspire or restrict your passionate interest in any area of specific creative endeavor? If so, how?

Definitive statements and assessments about your creative expression have a potent effect, for better or worse. Professor of Art Education and author David London wrote, "All statements marking good and bad, like and dislike, in some fashion damage our spirit and consequently lead us to pull on our defensive armor. This is a terribly steep price to pay for what is actually desired in the exchange: increased capacity for breadth of imagination and clarity of expression." If we lacked encouragement, especially in our formative years, there is a good chance our creativity was stunted.

Whatever detrimental effects there may be from your past, however stymied you may feel in your creative endeavors, you *can change*. To desire more creativity is a start. If you reflect on returning to an area of creative interest, that is movement. As we back that reflection with focused intention, it will eventually come to pass. Creativity is your birthright and is always there for you, however obscured it may be.

Make a Dream List

Make a dream list of those creative areas that you would like to expand. Prioritize the top two areas. Do not hesitate to list interests in which you have had no previous experience. If you have always wanted to play a musical instrument, put it down on the list even if you feel intimidated by the prospect. Give yourself permission to try a new area. How will you build confidence by refusing to begin and to try? Here are some suggestions for creating your dream list:

1. **Unleash your imagination**: Give yourself permission to name your dreams, identify your hopes, desires and what you believe will make you happy. Remember, creativity has no limits.

2. **Identify areas of creative interest**: What interested you as a child? Were you drawn to color, or fantasy, dance or mechanics? Be sure not to censor any area because you believe it's impractical.

3. **Creativity is an experiment in expanding awareness**: Select a couple of areas in which you desire to begin creative exploration.

4. **As you see yourself, so you become**: Imagine yourself successfully, joyously working in the areas of interest you just identified. As you imagine, you cast a blueprint of the future which has the power to become manifest.

5. **Set aside time**: Structure some time to begin exploring and working with these interests.

6. **Dynamic intention:** With focused intention, visualize and affirm your creativity.

7. **Integrate creativity into daily life:** Let creativity enliven your work, family, romantic and spiritual life. Every aspect can benefit from the creative flair within.

Giving Yourself Permission to Change

Have you ever wondered what gets in the way of claiming your own happiness? If happiness is so important, why isn't it easier to attain? One reason is that the Limited Self becomes attached to its own limitation. Human nature tends to hold on to what is familiar, even if it is confining or brings discontent. Before any change can happen, you must give yourself permission to release those parts that resist change. You must embrace your worthiness to succeed. Resistance to new endeavors clips the wings upon which your creativity can soar heaven-bound.

By giving yourself permission to change, imagination will stir and gain momentum to move along new lines. The commitment to change and open to your creativity must precede any effective thrust of will.

Will is the energetic spark that ignites all worthy endeavors. To desire without energy, to desire without vision, is to invite stagnation and reduce the possibilities of full claiming. You must first place your intention upon your creative desires. Intention will begin to stir dynamic will-based energy. Intention is your broadcast to the Divine and to the divinity within and will summon response from the universal divine energy that is ever supporting your endeavors. Your unfolding and expansion is of vital interest to the Source of all.

Becoming Fearless

Perhaps you harbor fears about undertaking new creative efforts. If so, you might ask yourself, "What is the worst thing that can happen to me if I try and do not succeed?" You are redefining yourself as a risk-taker by taking action in spite of the fear. Learning to take risks will expand access to your creativity.

Once you have given yourself permission to change and to redefine yourself as a creative being, you will need to keep reminding yourself of your commitment. As you embrace positive

> *Once you make a decision, the universe conspires to make it happen.*
> RALPH WALDO EMERSON

change wholeheartedly, you begin a process that opens you to the Universal Flow. You find yourself supported by powerful forces of the Universe. You ignite the creative force within, and blaze with new possibilities. Your true artistry is born.

Regardless of your particular habit patterns, feelings of unworthiness, lack of self confidence or negative self talk, if you continue to make the effort, you will be victorious. Be patient! If the pace of your progress disappoints you, keep moving toward change anyway.

History is filled with inspiring examples of artists who persevered despite great odds. In 1913 when Igor Stravinsky debuted his now famous *Rite of Spring*, audiences rioted. Yet it was this very work that changed the way composers in the 20th century thought about music; the work cemented his place in musical history. Today Monet's paintings sell for millions of dollars and hang in some of the most prestigious institutions in the world. Yet during his own time, his work was mocked and rejected by the artistic elite, the Paris Salon. Monet kept at his impressionist style, which caught on and became a starting point for major changes to art that helped usher in the modern era.

Had either Stravinsky or Monet lacked patience and perseverance, or succumbed to negative or self-defeating thoughts, the world would never have been graced with their unique artistic expression. Their examples, and many others, should encourage you in your efforts to free yourself from self doubt. Much like the onion that is formed in layers, your layers of false thoughts must be peeled away, one by one, in order for you to shed them. Acts of change and empowerment begin with permission to change, redefine yourself, and imagine.

Change Maker

Crafter of Subtle forms,
Image Maker,
Carver of magnificent edifices,
Sculptor of Light,
Architect of Monuments,
You created it All,
You took the first step to change.

Then the heavens bowed to meet you.
O' Change Maker,
Creator of forms,
Artisan of possibilities,
You took the first step to change.

Then the Heavens bowed to meet you.

CREATIVITY AND IMAGINATION

Creativity and imagination are synergistic. Imagination inspires creativity and forms the seed thoughts that are then cultivated into myriad outer expressions of creativity. *Creativity begets more creativity.* The more you unleash its latent power, the more you have. The more you have, the more unbounded is its expression in you.

To imagine is to cast an image into a light form by using your mind. The more you exercise imagination, the greater the potential for creating seed thoughts and direct creative expressions. To imagine means that you are

> *Creativity is our true nature; blocks are an unnatural thwarting of a process at once as normal and as miraculous as the blossoming of a flower at the end of a slender green stem.*
>
> JULIA CAMERON,
> *The Artist's Way*

a painter in the light, and a sculptor and form maker in the light. Nothing will materialize without the light image being cast first. The source of that imagination is Spirit—a vast sea of limitless Spirit. As you use your mental abilities in this way, you are remaking your life, accessing creative power, and unlocking the potency and the potential of who you truly are.

Creativity and Love

An energized heart is a creative heart. An energized heart is expansive in loving. By contrast, stagnation of energy in the heart center diminishes the creative flow. If you would expand your creativity, you must increase your loving.

To live in the love vibration is to activate the heart center. The heart expands by the act of giving. It is out of love and union that creativity expresses itself in the highest way with the conception of a child. From seed energy, the embryo is formed, and from the embryo, the baby is born. When love is in the heart of the mother and father, that very vibration enters into the seed (the ovum/sperm). Through love, creation occurs. Through continuous loving, creation is enhanced.

To encourage greater creativity in life, love more, give more, and serve more, selflessly. This loving, giving, and serving will further create an alignment between the Limited and Eternal Selves. The greater the alignment, the more you will experience congruency with your deeper nature and with the flow of life itself. This is the key to manifesting your dreams. All of these elements are involved in energizing the heart. Loving is the key to this expansion.

One method of activating the heart center is to concentrate on the spine and consciously bring energy from the lower section of the spinal column near the tailbone, up toward the dorsal area of the spine opposite the heart. Once the energy has been centered in the heart center, broadcast the energized feeling outward in expanding waves of love. This technique is widely used by adherents of Yoga and many other spiritual paths to develop love and compassion.

CREATIVITY: THE LIMITED SELF AND THE ETERNAL SELF

If you believe creativity is primarily an expression of the Limited Self, then creativity, by its nature, is limited. This narrow vantage point ties you to your physical, psychological identity in the material world. From the perspective of the Limited Self, not only is supply limited, but manifestation has finite restriction. Belief in finite restriction significantly stunts the expression of creativity.

For the Limited Self, creativity combines skill sets, specific abilities, and/or attributes. If you measure your personal worthiness in this way, you will perceive limitations in your capacity to express creativity. Your creativity then becomes limited, tied to faulty self-definitions and issues of deservedness.

CREATIVITY AND THE ETERNAL SELF

Creativity, as viewed from the vantage point of the Eternal Self, is another thing entirely. You not only possess, but are a powerhouse that can tap the dynamic force of creation itself. The nature of the Eternal Self is beyond any limit whatsoever.

Let us look at possibilities of creativity from the perspective of the Eternal Self, which knows its lineage is with the Creator of all. It is incapable of experiencing the idea of separation from the Creator. The inward diving into those still waters of Spirit will harvest the pearls of that Self in all their luminous glory. In the silence, creativity flows. In the imagination, creativity flourishes. In will-directed activity, creativity manifests.

As you increase your alignment within yourself, the Limited and Eternal Selves enter into harmony and thus, greater authenticity. There is no "pretend" or presumption. The ego-based personality falls away, giving birth to a more refined, integrated being. You sense a new centeredness within your core nature—the soul—which naturally aligns with the limitless universe and the power and force of creation itself.

The Passion of Suffering versus the Passion of Joy

Whatever the form of artistic expression, whether it is painting, music, writing, poetry, dance, etc., there are those who believe that suffering is necessary. This popular misconception—that artistic expression requires nearly unbearable sacrifice and suffering—has been fueled by images of tormented artists throughout history and in contemporary culture. True artistic passion can exist in suffering. But passion can exist as well in divine expression and joy.

While some have managed to create great art from their suffering, deep and great agony rarely translates into enduring artistic endeavors. Suffering and joy are not static, but move as energy lines in creation. They also generate either a negative flow of energy or a positive flow of energy in the universal flow. How you experience passion, with either suffering or joy, creates in you a legacy of consciousness habits. If you are interested in having your artistic expression emanate from joy, then you should consider developing a greater alignment with the Eternal Self.

For some, of course, art flows out of a deep sense of joy, love, abundance and the desire to express and share their creative gifts. For others, the idea that a joy-filled consciousness can create deeply felt art may be challenging. However, passion is present in both creation and in destruction. Passion exists in polarity. Where and how you channel that passion, will determine, to some degree, how you move those lines of energy. Remember that these moving lines of energy also have the power of magnetism and attraction. The movement of energy continues to operate by the law of attraction, whether it is criticized, rejected, exalted or embraced. How you participate in your passion brings forth new lines of magnetic attraction.

A kind of happiness may be based upon self-indulgence of the Limited Self. Joy, on the other hand, is the domain of the Eternal Self. Except with a Christ-like figure of true spiritual stature, suffering cannot uplift the consciousness of others or yourself. Suffering, without enlightenment, can simply be an invitation for others to join in shared misery.

The passion of joy also can also emanate from and continue resonating from within the universe itself. The passion of suffering, on the other hand, continues to emanate, but that emanation ties you to a negative flow of energy. With an effort to access more of your joy-filled nature, you can tap into and experience creativity to the fullest. Whether you desire to express the passion associated with suffering or the passion associated with joyous expansion is up to you.

If you desire greater self-integration, you will discover that the universe is on tap for your wildest dreams. Creativity is not limited to your earthly experiences, but also contains the primordial energy of all experience, all passion, and all joy. The Source of creativity within you is brimming with possibilities and always ready to support, encourage and inspire you. Aligned with it, your discoveries are transcendent and illuminating, for you were born to be a creator.

Creativity: We unleash it. We don't acquire it

Your real power is not in the acquisition of creativity, but in the unlocking and unleashing of the dormant power of the Creator within. This occurs when you open to your divine nature. You express more creativity when you:

- Claim creativity as your birthright.
- Explore your dreams and inspirations.

- Make time for creative endeavors.
- Journal as a creative tool. (A good resource is *The Artists' Way* by Julia Cameron.)
- Become more aware/conscious of what holds you back and work on reversing those thoughts/behaviors.
- Visualize and affirm creativity.

Exploring your Dreams as Sources of Inspiration and Creativity

No dream can manifest without first allowing yourself to dream. What are your most precious dreams? What are the hopes and desires you want to experience? The dreams you dream in your waking state are the hopes and desires that you long to achieve. Explore these ideas, desires and urges.

Perhaps there are new areas of creative expression that you are curious about. No image can take form without the imagination. No energy can be moved forward by sheer willpower alone. You must first have the framework for it. See yourself as a powerful creator capable of recasting old roles and manufacturing new mental movie scripts in which you are more joyous, happy, and creatively expressive.

To do this, invite imagination to a new level. Envision that you are an actor creating the script of your life on the big screen. Mentally cast yourself in a creative role. What does that part look like? Does it involve a high level of performance with a specific skill? Or do you see the actor exhibiting definite attributes? Is there a specific talent, or area of mastery, you long desired to explore, exhibit, or perform? Let your imagination open fully, without entertaining any limitation. What would your life look like if you were absolutely assured of success?

To increase your capacity to imagine, practice visualizing the various roles. Combining the visualization with the successful emotional feeling state will intensify the experience. Giving form to dreams, making them concrete in your imagination, and feeling the experience *as if it were real*, will further stimulate the creative process. The time to begin is now. We must not only give ourselves permission to dream, but cast ourselves as the star performer in our personalized dream-script.

Write down your thoughts and feelings in a journal for exploring your dreams. You will only be able to explore which dreams are worth pursuing when you are fully clear about what they are.

To Dream Your Dreams, Avoid Mind-Altering Chemicals

Many habitual users of mind-altering substances believe that their hopes, desires, and dreams are more powerful and more imaginative because of the use of chemicals, drugs, or marijuana.

However, chemicals that may stimulate the flow of ideas can also paralyze the power of will to move those ideas forward. Such substances hamper the development of self-discipline. They impair the focus and direction of the energy needed to activate will power.

Creativity requires the combination of inspiration and imagination with will-based activity. At some point, thoughts and ideas must be propelled forward by concentration and dynamic will. No matter how beautiful the automobile, it will not go far without a fully functioning engine. Marijuana, among other substances, kills initiative, drive, and action. It dulls ambition and seduces the user into simply dreaming the dreams with no follow through.

There are no short cuts in the effort to materialize a creative life. Imagination does not originate in chemicals, but rather stirs in the sea of Spirit and creation. Your focused intention allows you to ride the waves of inspiration and imagination in that limitless sea. Chemicals may promise oceanic experiences, but actually bind and tie users to the shores of stagnation. Regular use of marijuana and other mind-altering substances may provide the illusion of creating experiences without actualizing them in everyday life.

An interiorized consciousness (achieved through quality meditation techniques) expands consciousness. Sedating consciousness does not interiorize it. Sedation can also create a dependence upon the substance, if not chemically, then psychologically. Meditation, with quality techniques, is a superior pathway to knowing and experiencing the creative.

Dreams During the Sleep State Enhance Creativity

The pre-sleep state and actual dream experiences are powerful tools to enhance your creativity.

- Your dream life is positive proof of the power of your imagination and the gift of your inherent creativity. Your "storytelling" and image-making while asleep exhibit unbounded creativity. This should encourage you in re-defining yourself as imaginative, inspired, and creative.

- Your dream life may also function as a spiritual compass. The Eternal Self may use the language and symbols of dreams to inspire you toward greater self-knowledge and integration. The Eternal Self encourages the consciousness toward greater joy, self-knowing, and love.

- Your dreams provide a mirror of your habits of consciousness and your deepest attitudes.

Pre-sleep suggestions can allow the cycle of dreaming and sleep to improve your ability to engage in those positive behaviors when awake. Pre-sleep suggestions can incubate creative ideas and encourage your receptivity to information beyond the domain of the Limited Self. When you visualize and affirm positive suggestions as you fall asleep, you deepen your access to the universal unconscious, the God-stream of knowing. The border between waking and sleep is a powerful state. This affirmation can help tap its potential: "I give thanks, for in the sleeping state, clarity comes to me about my higher purpose, and the greatest positive use of my energy."

Many of us have never fully explored our life's higher purpose. Jobs allow us to earn income to meet obligations, but they are often not congruent with our true purpose. A higher life purpose must align with the soul's nature and the best use of time, energy, resources, and possibilities.

Are your current roles carved out by default? Have you, perhaps, been attempting to live someone else's dream? Although you have an obligation to your present circumstances, this does not mean you cannot explore other meaningful, creative aspects of life and work. If you desire greater peace, joy, and happiness, you must allow yourself to explore, imagine, and create. Such exploration does not exempt you from duty, responsibility, and attention to those dependent upon you. Yet despite such roles, you are not limited in your capacity to explore your creativity.

Your preconceptions about your identity are powerfully guarded and influenced by the ego. It readily goes into either assaultive or defensive modes of resistance, when new ideas challenge preconceptions. As you enter the pre-sleep state, the ego-based consciousness becomes less vigilant.

On the other hand, the Eternal Self has no need to defend its expansiveness in truth and in the vibration of love. The Eternal Self is simply in a state of perfect Being. Pre-sleep suggestions that resonate with the truth of the soul will guide you to response and action.

Any suggestion in the pre-sleep state will act as a stimulus for experiencing the Eternal Self. An affirmation which states, "When I sleep, I create" gives permission and direction to the subconscious to bring into your experience your most desired goals and needs.

The greater the alignment and attunement between the Limited Self and the Eternal Self, the greater will be the possibility of changing impermanent states of happiness to enduring states of joy.

The technique of auto-suggestion involves these simple steps:

- Envision white light around you and give thanks that you are divinely protected and divinely inspired by the power and the force of the universe, or God. (Petition a power higher than yourself in whatever manner makes you comfortable.)
- After you have mentally surrounded yourself with white light, state that ideas of inspiration and creativity are now manifesting. Possible affirmations that could be used are:

My mind incubates the creative flow.
My mind is inspired with creative solutions.
I am inspired by powerful, creative solutions in my career life and in my personal life.
Spirit inspires solutions that come to me with clarity while in the dreaming and sleeping state.
I am creative mind. I am inventive mind. I access knowing. I penetrate truth. I am inspired by the Infinite Thought.

In this pre-sleep state, continue to repeat any of these sentences, or other similar ideas, while focusing your energy on the screen of your forehead, at the point between the eyebrows ("spiritual eye"). Proceed with intention and receptivity, as if it is inevitable that you will receive a divine positive response. Your consciousness should not entertain doubts about your capacity to receive or create.

Keep a notebook, or paper and pencil, near your bedside to assist you in recording thoughts, ideas, or inspirations that may come to you in that resting or sleeping state. Develop the habit of writing down these thoughts; this will encourage your focus of intention and your ability to receive inspiration. Thoughts not written down or recorded may rapidly disappear. If you continue with this practice night after night, you will find that sleep incubates creative thought.

You can also do affirmations around specific creative areas, such as music, writing, and art. After you have mentally placed the white light of protection around yourself, then mentally repeat, "I am inspired in my music, art, writing, etc. The power of inspiration and creativity are manifesting in magnificent form now." Another affirmation:

As I sleep, I create.
As I sleep, I invent.
As I sleep, I solve all problems.

> *If the consciousness can think and dream itself into bad habits, it has only to think and dream differently to form good habits. Good or bad ideas are different forms or different dreams of consciousness. It is better to dream beautiful phases of consciousness than to have nightmares. Consciousness is imaginative, sensitive, and pliable; it can think and dream itself into any state.*
>
> PARAMAHANSA YOGANANDA
> *God Talks with Arjuna, pg. 34*

Time Management

The subject of time management may appear to be directly opposite the concept of creative flow. Many feel that creative flow moves with the greatest force if unhampered or unrestricted by humanity's artificial constraints. But even the most powerful river is contained on either side as it moves toward the ocean. "Containing" (managing) your time is essential if your creative flow is to move toward its fullest, most oceanic expression. Providing the proper time and place for your creativity is necessary, just as it is for any worthy endeavor.

A tempting way of avoiding your fears regarding creativity is to hide your potential behind the excuse of having no time. You must build in some structured time to exercise your creativity if it is to expand.

In reality, the more you are centered and aligned with yourself, the greater your access to inspiration, and the more connected you are to the stream of all creation. The more fragmented you are, the less consistent is your access to that stream. You can train your pliable consciousness to become more imaginative by exercising your imagination.

The habit that we are attempting to cultivate, above all, is the habit of discipline. Discipline is directly tied to will-based intentions. Discipline strengthens will. Through discipline you can train the consciousness to increasingly imagine and visualize. When you set aside time just to imagine success in creative endeavors and to practice the habit of gratitude, you will reinforce the spiritual quality of gratitude and the habit of creativity by aligning more fully with the Creator.

You have probably experienced the desire to try something new — to paint, or to take up a musical instrument, or write your memoir. Perhaps procrastination set in, and before you knew it, another year, or two, went by. There is no time like the present to begin. This requires discipline. Discipline helps us to persevere. Thomas Edison is supposed to have said, "All great ideas are 10% inspiration and 90% perspiration." Time management is critical to the cultivation of discipline and, hence, to expressing your creativity.

Discipline is also especially important in a spiritual practice, such as meditation, an essential component to a happy, creative life. Meditation is more than just a way of relaxing and entering into a heightened state of peace. Peace does not just happen by chance, nor does accessing creativity. It is the cultivated outcome of disciplined practice. The more you meditate with keen attention, the more consistently you are able to access deeper states of consciousness. And the deeper you go into consciousness, the more your creative channel opens. Adding meditation to your daily routine can dramatically speed the progress of your creative journey.

How to be Manage Your Time More Effectively

- Analyze how you use your time. Write down how your time is spent each day, analyzing patterns.
    - a) Work activities.
    - b) Recreational activities.
    - c) Non-work activities: reading, the Internet, TV.
- Include creative activities each day. View this "appointment" with yourself as a gift—of play and reconnection with your spirit and essence.
- Set small goals at first. Giving yourself short periods of time to work on specific projects can be a way of increasing skill and refining the use of time. Even 15-30 minutes a day will develop the habit of creativity.
- Set quality time. Spend at least 15-30 minutes a day seeing yourself as inventive, happy, grateful for your creative nature.
- Keep a Journal. Writing about your dreams and goals makes them more real and signals to the subconscious mind that you are serious about change. The process of writing creates greater commitment. You should be sure to include any non-practical ideas and goals. That is, do not omit things that you think cannot come true. By judging hope and creativity as non-practical, you stifle yourself. Include practical steps to explore creative interests.
- Prioritize Activities. You can always find the time to do the things that are important to you. If you have time to sit and read a newspaper, a magazine, or watch a television show, you have some time available to devote to creative projects.
- Find balance. A balanced life restores your energy and allows for even more inspiration. Excessive work results in imbalance.

If you have a demanding work schedule, you will need to relax or unwind after the busy-ness of activities. This is necessary. Too often, however, you may go from excessive activity to excessive loafing.

You have surely heard the term "workaholic." Do you have these tendencies? If so, think about the consequences to your life and happiness. Preoccupation with work, without inner exploration of one's self, and failure to prioritize meaningful relationships, will produce one-sidedness and disharmony.

You more easily become attached to your roles when you identify with the Limited Self, which has no sense of self beyond the parameters of worldly and role-related activities. This is how the small self perceives, measures and presents itself. The Eternal Self, on the other hand, does not identify with roles. It is pure being, pure consciousness. If locked into the smallness of the Limited Self, your awareness becomes narrower. You don't feel inspired to explore your inner being.

Embarking on the journey of discovering yourself as creative being is a vital step towards further alignment between the two selves and tapping into the creative aspect of all life and all creation.

Journaling as a Creative Tool

As mentioned elsewhere, journaling is the technique of writing down your thoughts and feelings without censoring your ideas. It involves allowing free-flowing thoughts, emotions and ideas to be what they are, unhindered. Ideas, thoughts, and grammar are not to be arranged and edited with a reader in mind. Such free writing will give you greater clarity about yourself and lead to meaningful self-dialogue.

Keeping a journal handy makes it easier to develop the habit of writing down thoughts upon awakening or retiring. It is important to have a time for self-reflection at least twice a day for 15-20 minutes. It is in this free flow writing process that the consciousness becomes more transparent. Journaling is a wonderful tool of self-discovery and can increase your communication with yourself, allowing you to experiment with imagination and dreams: the dreams you live in the present and the dreams you long to express.

Journaling may also be used to clarify creative goals and map out the pathways to achieve them. To be successful, you begin by identifying and setting small, attainable goals with a projected timeline that is realistic. Then give yourself permission to begin. If you are interested in art, scheduling a time for yourself to walk around an art store is an excellent beginning. Another goal could be that you ask for information on a good book for a beginner. You may want to pursue information on classes or books and material available in an area that you have previously pursued. Develop strategies that make it feel more real to begin to investigate areas of interest. Some areas to explore when journaling:

a. List three areas of artistic or creative expression that you have wanted to try, expand, or revisit.

b. When considering new or past areas of creativity, what concerns, anxieties or fears come up for you? Fears of failure? Or are there fears about what would happen if you did succeed?

c. Is the thought of significant change frightening to you? Why? How would change interfere with your self-image? How does the idea of change impact your deservedness issues?

d. Are you able to give yourself permission to play with your creativity? Or are you fixated on the final outcome of your creative expression?

e. Have you had an idea or plan that you felt may have some practical value? Do you credit yourself as being someone who has creative ideas?

f. Do you have the idea for an invention, or a modification of something that has already been marketed? Do you feel it might be worth pursuing any creative or inventive ideas?

g. List three areas in which you would like to express more creativity in the *practical* areas of your life, i.e., career, projects such as reorganizing home or office, or creative modification as a problem-solving tool.

h. Identify ways of approaching creative interests that would give you greater permission to explore. How can you give yourself permission to begin?

Becoming More Self-Aware

Journaling enhances introspection and improves the quality of your self-dialogue. You cannot change what you do not know. Journaling will allow you to visit your fears—both those that are known and those that lie deeper, buried in your unconscious. Writing can help to objectify areas of emotional difficulty and blockages that we all experience. This will give you a greater feeling of control over your life.

Do not underestimate the power of self-knowledge. You cannot uproot tenacious fear energy without first identifying it. As Socrates wrote, "The unexamined life is not worth living." By bringing in the light of understanding, the "darkness" of your fears becomes illumined. Only then can you release them.

> *We pay a heavy price for our fear of failure. It is a powerful obstacle to growth. It assures the progressive narrowing of the personality and prevents exploration and experimentation. There is no learning without some difficulty and fumbling.*
>
> JOHN W. GARDNER

If you do not explore your creativity, is the reason for this fear-based? If so, the first step in overcoming this fear is becoming aware of its presence and influence. Fear related to your creative energy may simply be due to the habit of self-negation or feelings of unworthiness. You can look at this tendency through the new lens of understanding. This broader perspective allows you to confront those issues more clearly, identifying their root cause and eliminating them from your life. Always keep in mind that habit patterns in consciousness may become your destiny. Every effort to bring them to light and to eradicate those that do not serve you brings you one step closer to freedom and creative self-expression. Consciousness, energy and manifestation are intrinsically linked.

By the use of imagination, permission to change, renewed intention and inspiration, you create a new destiny. May that new destiny contain more of your innate creative potential. The re-awakening of creativity presents keys that will open new doors of self-esteem and self-valuing. You gain more access to the truth of your own nature by the alignment of the Limited and Eternal Selves. With that increased merging, you tap into the dynamo of powerful creation itself. As you become more aware of the Creator within, you experience the Creator without. You are a dynamic, powerful creator, connected with the power of all creation.

Obstacles to Claiming Your Creative Self

If you look closely within, you will see that there are two main obstacles to accessing your creative self: the fear of failure and the fear of success. Behind most creative blocks is either one or the other. Many times one of these fears will manifest in the form of a paralyzing creative block that does not allow us to produce or achieve consistent follow-through with creative efforts. Sometimes we choose to do nothing rather than risk failure or success. This strategy often emerges to protect the self from others' judgments, assessments, and criticisms.

How you choose to participate in your own creativity is consistent with how your consciousness views your deservedness or worthiness. Fear proceeds from deep in the unconscious. You may be unaware of its cause. This is why journaling is vital. If you are to manifest your own special gifts and talents, it is essential that you uproot the causes of constrictions that prevent you from exploring your creative nature.

Fear of Failure

Fear of failure is something most of us, at some time or another, have experienced. This may be especially true when it comes to your creativity, for creativity involves exposing deeper parts of yourself. Expressing yourself may make you feel vulnerable.

As with the fear of success, the fear of failure can involve some level of psychological projection. What exactly is psychological projection? In Freudian psychology, *psychological projection* or *projection bias* is a defense mechanism. According to Wikipedia, it occurs when "a person unconsciously denies their own attributes, thoughts, and emotions, which are then ascribed to the outside world, such as to the weather, a tool, or to other people. Thus, it involves imagining or *projecting* that others have those feelings."

Said in another way, all that we perceive outside the self is a mirror of something within us. Everything that we see outside is a 'projection'. We project our energy, both positive and negative, onto other people and assume it is within them, often denying that it is within us. When we feel unworthy, at fault, or inadequate, we may keep those feelings unconscious, redirecting (or "projecting") them onto another.

Does this come into play with your fears around creativity? If you are not aware of your own internal dynamics, assumptions and projections, you can easily mislead yourself into thinking that there is "truth" in your lack of creative ability. You may assume that others do not find you capable, talented, filled with potential or worthy of success. This type of projection, an inaccurate assessment of yourself, can keep you locked in faulty self-definition.

Furthermore, if you received no validation or encouragement of your creative efforts as a child, you may have gone through life without a solid sense of self, afraid to take risks in creative expression. You may lack confidence and, having low self-esteem, you may project that others, too, have no faith in your abilities. This can turn into a self-fulfilling prophecy: you unconsciously create situations in which people do not support you so that you "validate" these feelings of unworthiness.

Early experiences of shame, embarrassment, and unworthiness, may have come throughout your life, triggered by events, relationships, or the inner movement of consciousness as unresolved issues surfaced. Fears of being exposed as untalented arise. Projection then validates your own faulty self-perception.

These themes of worthiness and deservedness are powerful and can subtly adopt various forms that show up as life obstacles. Assessing your own worth by the perceived opinions of others leaves you vulnerable and stuck in a cycle of helplessness. For many, the fear of failure thwarts, or can permanently thwart even minimal efforts at expressing creativity.

"IN ALL THY GETTING, GET UNDERSTANDING."

The good news is that your awareness of these principles alone can be liberating. Awareness is the birth of understanding. Journaling, along with the other practices described especially in the Stepping Stones to Change chapter of this book, can give you the power to stand firm in the face of fear and not be overwhelmed by it or succumb to a distorted perception of the self.

Part of the remedy when confronting fear of failure is the practice of self-dialogue and self-exploration. You have to remain ever mindful of the negative self-talk that echoes as loud chatter, berating and diminishing your own capabilities. Conscious attention to self-dialogue, and developing the habit of journaling to clarify mental processes, allows the creative process to expand. Such practices will also help you dissolve the shadows you cast upon your own creative process.

Your ultimate goal is to gain greater alignment with and integration of the Limited and Eternal Selves. The more you do this, the more your negative self talk will cease, and the less power the negativity of others will have over you. You will dramatically decrease your own struggles with worthiness and deservedness as you shift your identity to a much larger and more accurate assessment of yourself.

Regardless of your fears and struggles, change is always possible. Each effort you make on the path of life strengthens your confidence and self-knowing. If you have a solid enough sense of self, the opinions of others will not deter you from your creative endeavors. Failures will not devastate you. They may discourage you, surely, and you may be hurt by them, but you will not internalize them so deeply that they become your reality. Your natural urge to express your innate curiosity about life will propel you forward despite any lack of positive reinforcement. If you believe that you deserve good things to happen, you will take the risk to express your creative nature.

Often the desire to achieve public attention and fame from creative efforts is an expression of the need for love and approval that was not experienced in childhood. With sufficient admiration, you may assume that you will feel loved. But without self-validation and feelings of self-love, no audience will be sufficiently large to fill the internal void. Developing contentment within the self, and giving yourself permission to learn, explore and try new things without external approval are necessary to release the fear of failure.

Fear of Success

We can all relate to the fear of failure, but perhaps not so readily to the fear of success. If we take a deeper look at this fear, however, perhaps it, too, may have had an influence on your life.

Have you ever felt timid about exposing your talents or your deeper self to others? Have you ever entertained the thought that being successful might represent change, and that change might be painful? Would you open yourself more to others' criticism, rejection or ridicule? Any number of such thoughts and feelings may lie beneath the surface of your awareness, influencing or thwarting your efforts.

Perhaps you harbor an underlying fear that you are not worthy of success. If that fear exists, even unconsciously, you may feel safer remaining where you are and not trying something new. The core thought of being unworthy of success has enormous power. It may hide unrecognized behind thoughts such as: "Your success is a fluke. You will never be able to repeat this success or be applauded for your creativity again." Or "You know, you don't deserve the recognition. In the end, people will discover you are a fraud."

If you believe that success is a good thing, on the other hand, and that it won't hurt or alienate you from others, that you are, deep down, deserving of all good, then you won't be afraid or blocked.

Shifting the Cycle of Negativity

Ideas of unworthiness, feelings of inadequacy, and negative self-talk, underlie both fears of failure and fears of success. Negative self-talk constructs powerful walls that stifle and curtail the creativity within. From this day forward, affirm your creative nature. As you do, you will begin to pull down those walls. Give yourself full permission to step into a new level of creative expression.

Strategies to confront fear of failure or success:

- Increase positive self-dialogue and self-analysis.
- Analyze habit patterns of consciousness: As we think, so we create.
- Journal about fears related to both success and failure.
- Be willing to be a beginner.
- Focus on the journey; avoid preoccupation with the outcome.

- Affirm the creative power within; intend to explore and expand it.
- Experiment with, or learn, new areas of interest.
- Schedule time for creativity.
- Exercise imagination by allowing creative inspiration to flow.
- Give thanks in affirmations for the unfolding of divine creativity.
- Practice meditation. Emphasize Aum technique of Self-Realization Fellowship (available through a home-study course, Self-Realization Fellowship; 3880 San Rafael Avenue; Los Angeles, California 90065-3219.)
- Visualize being involved in successful, creative endeavors.
- Mentally give thanks for this creative aspect of life.
- Be creative in problem-solving and using inventive consciousness.
- Utilize positive visualizations as well as affirmations.
- Practice affirmations on creativity and worthiness to confront deservedness issues and invite the expansion of your creativity.

Creativity begins with small steps that are within reach. If you have always wanted to paint, for example, be willing to learn some basics in drawing or sketching. Try to learn the principles involved in depicting light, shadow and perspective from a book or a class. (An excellent book on art is *Drawing from the Right Side of Your Brain,* by Betty Edwards.) Or if you've always wanted to play or write music, be willing to learn the basics.

> *The spiritual law of reciprocity determines that what we give out returns to us. If we give out goodness, goodness will return to us and vice versa.*

Visualize yourself doing creative activities, feeling relaxed and successful.

Be willing to be a beginner! So many people lament that they are not masters of a particular artistic form. But all true masters in any field started as beginners. There is no shame in having no previous experience. There is, however, great sadness in not giving yourself permission to try.

Throughout this book you will notice references to the importance of giving yourself permission to change. Underneath this permission is the faith that you *can* change and that the Universe will *support* you when you try. Once given, that permission will open your creativity in ways that are boundless, limitless. Simply giving yourself permission will move your life and your energy with inspiration and imagination along new lines of creativity.

> *Let your mind start a journey through a strange new world. Leave all thoughts of the world you knew before. Let your soul take you where you long to be...Close your eyes. Let your spirit start to soar and you'll live as you've never lived before.*
>
> ERICH FROMM

Finding Your Creative Pulse — A Visualization

Begin by breathing deeply. Deep breathing relaxes the mind and body and provides more oxygen to the brain for clearer thought and higher creativity. Always come back to your breathing. Is it shallow, or are you breathing freely? Ask yourself: *"What would I really love to do?"* or *"What have I been longing to do—for years?"* Dare to imagine your new possibilities. Your passion is a guiding light—showing you bright new possibilities in your personal and professional life.

Imagine yourself being given one wish that is guaranteed to come true. If you could do anything in the world, and if success were assured, what would you do? Let your consciousness roam in the limitless sea of possibilities. Follow the impulses of your heart and soul. Would you be a dancer? A pianist? A clothing designer? An inventor? Allow your imagination to explore the things you have always felt drawn to—your favorite colors, for example, or a beautiful garden setting. Be free to connect with whatever it is that most inspires your passion and interest.

During this exercise, project any images that come onto the movie screen of your imagination, focusing at the point between the eyebrows as if it were that screen. Begin the art of imagining and casting your desires into light forms of possibility. Focusing your attention with intention will stir your energy. Dynamic will energizes the scenes you imagined. Your mind can create what is now unimaginable. Your mind will etch creation into form. You are a creator!

Once your desires begin to manifest, make certain that they are aligned with spiritual principle. To gratify the self at the expense or detriment of others is not aligned with spiritual principle. Others have a right to their wants, needs, and desires. When you project your dreams, be certain that they will not be harmful, even unintentionally, to others.

Remember, the Limited Self can create energized attachment to the ideas and scenes it visualizes, so exercise discernment. Attachment to your desires also sends the Limited Self into another level, a flurry of activity that intensifies the desires, actions, and activities well-grounded in ego-based consciousness. This, then, diminishes your awareness of the Eternal Self. The desired objects, or experiences, become identified in your mind as being the source of your happiness. If this occurs, you lessen your desire to focus on greater integration with the Eternal Self.

The Joy is in the Journey

The joy is in the journey, not the destination. Happiness comes from reaching out to your dreams, tapping into your deepest heart and allowing life to fully express itself. If you believe that joy will only come to you if you have achieved a final destination, you will have minimized the journey. And it is in the journey that you expend your life energy and creativity and become a new force of creation. Joy results from attending to your consciousness at this moment in time. If you focus sufficient attention on attending to your consciousness, you will penetrate from the outer fabric of life into the innermost domain of Being. In doing so, you touch the Eternal Now and your nature is transformed.

Becoming preoccupied with the end product of the creative adventure robs you of pleasure in that process and can intensify fear of failure or success in the pursuit of creative endeavors. See your efforts as a gift of your time and energy to the universe. As Lord Krishna counsels in the *Bhagavad Gita*, "Do not attach to the results."

When you become preoccupied with the end result, the self-critical voice constricts creative flow. Say mentally or out loud:

I give this gift of my time, energy and effort to the universe.
I am aligned with my creative force and power.
Creative energy is flowing and expressing through me.

By placing your consciousness in the present moment, you align the Limited Self with the Eternal Self. The Limited Self darts between time sequences, as well as past and future events. Seldom, if ever, does the ego-driven, Limited Self, experience stillness in the now. Creativity is born in those moments of the now, not in the past and or the future.

When we are absorbed in creative effort, the world stops. We are, for those moments, outside of time, in the flow, living in the Eternal Now. The act of creation stops the push and pull of polarity and we experience the vastness of our creative self. We experience the stirring of Spirit itself. In that process the two selves align. And in that greater alignment we draw closer to the face of God and the mirror-reflection of our own divine nature.

Conclusion

You possess within your true nature a forceful creative dynamo that desires expression. That force wishes to be a co-participant with the divine Creator. When you were created, your consciousness was imbued with the principle of creativity. The very atoms of light danced into form. You are the power of that dream of Spirit. The stirring of imagination and thought energized into form underpins the expression of your being and your creativity.

You came into being by divine intention and the stirring of possibility. You, too, have the ability to stir creation into magnificent forms and dynamic images of infinite and varied possibilities. Be willing to dream your dreams. Blow breath into your dreams. Give your imagination the power of movement. Creation flows from your use of arrow-directed dynamic will, an electrified force field shimmering with every dream that could ever be entertained. Celebrate the inexhaustible possibilities! Go beyond any limiting ideas that diminish your life or the lives of others. Affirm your truth in order to claim your energy. The absolute power of creation resides within you. Tapping into and dynamically expressing that creative force is your birthright.

You were born out of the vision of God. The Creator of all instilled within you the power of creativity. The keys to the universe were placed in your hands and your right to the throne of creation was given to you as heir apparent. To bemoan your lack of talent or vision and your power as a creator is to denounce creation itself. Universes of possibilities move within you just as the heavenly bodies are rotating in divine perfection in deep space. May you capture the heavenly energy within and cast it into form.

CREATIVITY

True humility means to claim your oneness as a spark of that great overarching Spirit that is within all things. It means to accept what you have been given, The Gift of You.

The Gift of You

You are condensed starlight,
the sun and the moon of the universe.
You are a creator of divine sparks and emanations.
You are a carrier of the keys to the universe.

In your touch, hope awakens.
In your words, the sun shines brighter.
In your prayers, the moon softens the night.
And in your living, all the stars shine,
awakened from their sleep by your desires for knowing
and because you are.

To deny your Source or your abilities is neither humility nor accuracy of perception. The divine force of the universe has created you so that one day you will confidently claim your truth by penetrating into your light nature. You will feel the power within moving in joyous expression of self-knowing. All empowerment expresses true self-claiming. You will know yourself as Spirit moving in creation, unbounded by the flesh and the limitations of the world. You will know yourself as awake and alive in the Eternal Present! Your inspiration, imagination and flight with Spirit gives you universes to travel, wings to fly, and solar systems to explore.

Affirmations for Creativity

For Abundance through Creativity
Abundance and prosperity
are manifesting
through my creative endeavors
of will,
imagination,
and dynamic intention.

For Dynamic Co-creating
I am an instrument
of divine creativity.
I am a dynamic co-creator
with the universe.
Expansive, creative energy
is manifesting from me Now.

For Focus to Manifest Creativity
Night and day,
I am focused
in concentration.
My one-pointed focus
illumines all solutions
and dissolves all problems.
The power to create
is my birthright
manifesting.

For the Power to Create
The power to create
is expressing itself
through me.
Luminous possibilities
present themselves.
I capture the
thought bubbles
in my imagination.
My will-based initiative drives
the thought bubbles
into concrete manifestation.
Creativity shines,
reflecting
the luminous possibilities.

For Creative Power in the Light
I am the Light
of all suns.
I possess the power
of all creations.
My name is the name
of all Light,
all suns,
all power,
and all creations.

For Infinite Creative Possibilities
Abundance
and ever-new creativity
are mine Now,
expressing with infinite possibilities.

Blessings Abound
I contemplate.
I see and penetrate
into unceasing
and unending
blessings.
I bow in gratitude
and appreciation.
I stand tall
In accepting all blessings.

www.ingramcontent.com/pod-product-compliance
Lightning Source LLC
LaVergne TN
LVHW010317070426
835507LV00026B/3425